"We trained hard, but it seemed that every time we were beginning to form up into teams, we would be reorganized. I was to learn later in life that we tend to meet any new situation by reorganizing; and a wonderful method it can be for creating the illusion of progress while producing confusion, inefficiency, and demoralization."

. . . Gaius Petronius Arbiter, Roman Satirist, 210 BC.

While likely a false citation, it is at least known to have been said much later by Charlton Ogburn, Jr. (1911-1998).

It is not important who first uttered this cogent thought. When a business is not organized in such a way as to allow you to work efficiently and effectively, it has failed to make working what it should be. At the same time, when you don't clearly know what your work is, how to improve it, and how to work as an individual and within a team, both you and the business suffer. This book is designed to help you and the organization understand how to achieve optimal work and continuous improvement.

Danny Langdon
Originator of the Language of Work™
Business Consultant, 2018

THE MANAGING MODEL

FOR MANAGERS

THE MANAGING MODEL

USING THE LANGUAGE OF WORK TO FACILITATE WORK

BOOK 2 OF THE WORK TRILOGY

DANNY G. LANGDON
KATHLEEN S. LANGDON

Published by:
Performance International
5 Oval Court
Bellingham, WA 98229 USA
360-738-4010
www.performanceinternational.com
info@performanceinternational.com

ISBN Paperback: 978-0-9913975-8-7
ISBN eBook: 978-0-9913975-3-2

The Language of Work™

The Language of Work™ (LoW) is a systemic, enterprise-wide system for organizing, managing, implementing, and continuously improving work by means of powerful integration tools. This goal is achieved through the universal use of a Work Formula that is applied through a process known as Work Analytics to a series of integrated Work Implementation Models. While that sentence is a mouthful, this book turns it into a series of easily understood, illustrated pieces.

The anchor of the Language of Work is the Work Formula: a behaviorally based, clear reflection of work using a standard formula to apply various Work Analytic Tools. Its use allows:

- executive management to provide everyone with a shared understanding of the business mission, ultimate goals, and ongoing objectives;
- managers to effectively facilitate employee achievement; and
- workers to do their parts individually and in teams by thoroughly understanding work and committing to its continuous improvement and overall implementation.

Every business consists of people and jobs at all levels of the organization. Communication within and between these levels is paramount to business success. The three Work Implementation Models of the LoW are an excellent method of addressing this basic quality of business. A separate book is devoted to each one:

The Business Model

Primarily for executives, this book demonstrates how to organize a business to achieve work alignment, operational transparency, and continuous improvement. The model applies to all four levels where work is planned and accomplished. Ways to align organizational needs related to standards, work support, human relations, and financial support are also provided. The book is also recommended reading for managers and workers who want a complete understanding of the Language of Work as it relates their role in the business as a whole.

The Managing Model

Primarily for managers, including team leaders, this book explains how the Language of Work, through Work Analytic Tools, can facilitate various management functions to achieve continuous work improvements. The Managing Model is a logical, systemic extension of The Business Model. Thus, what the executive develops through The Business Model managers can effectively facilitate using the same Work Formula. The book will also be of interest to workers aspiring to a managerial role.

The Working Model

Primarily for workers, this book shows how to use the Language of Work Formula to implement and continuously improve work as an individual worker and as part of a team. Using a variety of Work

Analytic Tools, individuals and teams can work together to meet executive and management work goals. Using the Work Formula they learn how to continuously improve work to maximize work effectiveness, efficiency, and to effect needed changes as they are planned by management. Managers will want to read this book to support their facilitation of work.

Each of the three books in *The Work Trilogy* is written for a specific audience; each is independent, and yet all three comprise an integrated system. To make each book stand alone, a certain amount of redundancy is needed. We trust the reader of two or all three of the books will not find this bothersome. As with any new language, the Language of Work demands practice and repetition. Deeper insights can occur as one reads again, learning the many nuances of this new way to look at and practice the work of business.

As you learn new ways, the authors hope you will share that knowledge with us, and we welcome questions as you use the Language of Work.

Danny and Kathleen Langdon

The Managing Model: A Book for Managers

The first time I was assigned 28 people to manage, I was really not fully prepared. It wasn't that I didn't know my team or their work technically. I knew how to do my old job…in fact, that is why I was promoted: I was a great worker bee. But what I really didn't understand was the big picture: How did everyone's work—with all their different goals, functions, and skill sets—fit together? How could the business and I best support their accomplishing that work? How would I facilitate without doing their work for them? How on earth could I get everyone to agree on how the work should be accomplished as a team?

I am certain, having discussed the challenges of managing with hundreds of others since, I was not alone in such uncertainty. The feeling that I was managing by the seat of my pants weighed upon me, as well as on those I managed, and it took a long time for me to get comfortable. Still, I knew something was lacking. I knew I could do better! There surely must, I thought, have been a better way to organize my group, gain individual and shared understanding and commitment, and get great results.

Whether you are a new or experienced manager, you may, like me in those days, feel that managing can be done better. This book is written for you.

There are scads of books, seminars, training programs, and advice from others on the subject of work management. Talking heads expound, and electronic page-turners appear with the newest ways to management success. But all these start with a faulty assumption: that the work we will manage has been clearly defined and communicated, and that everyone equally shares that understanding.

Everyone surely understands what work is, because we all do work and plenty of it! But most management theory is somewhat abstract in that it often represents a good idea, process, and set of principles to be implemented. These are formulated by well-meaning thinkers and approached in theory, or as is often the case, as a vainly masked marketing effort by some consultant seeking to establish his or her place (and to mine your wallet). I hope you find that we are different, although we admit to some thoughts of financial incentive.

This book is unlike others on the principles and practices of managing. We are operationally based, having validated what we say by actual practice. We have been in many workplaces refining and proving our methodology. We make no untested assumptions.

This book is about establishing a *formula* for work—defining, operationally understanding, and clarifying work for everyone doing that work, as well as monitoring, improving, and measuring work for bonuses and performance appraisals. Once you have defined work in the way we suggest, you can excel as a manager, supervisor, team leader, or whatever your title, while you artfully facilitate the work of others under your care and guidance.

The Language of Work is a scientifically based behavioral model that has been tried and tested in many diverse workplaces over the last 25+ years. It was formulated by the author in the early '90s based on years of trying to improve the performances of individuals, groups, core processes, and the business as a whole. While the model is not yet taught in most AMA courses or MBA curricula, I think you will agree that it makes intuitive sense, has application to many other business needs, and is actually pretty easy to learn, use, and manage with others. Those we have introduced it to know that it makes sense, but more importantly that it is effective.

Until today, there has not been a tool that consistently lets you and others look at work the same way. It is as if there is now a new formula to relate every job to every process to every work group to every business unit . . . all using the same elements of work. Now missed deadlines can be examined without a need to assign blame. Now lost opportunities can be identified and exploited; now low engagement scores can be raised. Now the manager who is said to "play poorly with others" can be coached to produce good work as part of a team because he knows the work, can explain it to everyone and can facilitate it. Now the workers can know that their suggestions to improve work will be listened to.

Finally, just as with any new "language," it takes a while to become proficient. With repeated practice sharing the Language of Work with your workforce and other managers on a daily basis, you will find that you are doing "systems thinking" about work and its management. The results can be either subtle or dramatic, but there will be positive changes in your workplace and in your way of thinking about and managing the work of your enterprise.

Danny Langdon
Originator of the Language of Work
Performance International
5 Oval Court, Bellingham, WA 98229
www.performanceinternational.com

Contents

Acknowledgements

We want to thank several people for their generous time and thoughts in completing this book. First, my partner in life and business for her contributions, support, and ideas on assuring that this book was relevant to executives and managers. Special thanks to our copyeditor, Roby Blecker, as well as our final proofreader, Brittney Langdon, who checked consistency from book to book.

Thanks to several managers representative of those for whom we wrote the book. Their ideas and suggestions were instrumental in keeping the book centered on your needs and circumstances.

And special thanks to our "third-party" readers—Joanna Berg, Meg Lang, and Brenda Sample—who worked so diligently to find any last minute, glaring illustration or reading issues. Very special thanks to Ghislain Viau, Creative Publishing Book Design for working with us on cover designs, print and eBook formatting. With so many at-the-last minute edits and changes on three books at the same time he was very patient and extremely professional.

Danny and Kathleen Langdon

Preface

Everyone has their own perception of the work of an organization, and that is precisely the problem with work. One sees it by the org chart, others by function, or by the jobs and teams, and still others by the processes. Or worse yet, we only see the enterprise in terms of what we do. It's time for a common way to view business, understand how to improve it where needed, manage and do our work in concert with that shared understanding. That is where the Language of Work comes into play.

While we were writing this book, we often had conversations with a wide range of friends, colleagues and clients, who inquired about the subject of the book as part of the Trilogy of Work. As soon as we revealed the working title and basic content, the universal response was a not-so-unexpected, "Boy! Could my current (or former) company or department use this kind of systematic approach to understanding and organizing business!" Nearly everyone thinks businesses could be run better; they also agree that organizations are rarely defined and understood well. We have helped facilitate several organizations using the LoW and confirmed that it works. It will work for you!

Danny and Kathleen Langdon

Chapter 1

What Is Work?

Given that we all work—and a lot—it might seem to be odd to begin with the question, "What is work?" You would think that, from all our work experience, we must surely know what work is. Surprisingly, our experience with thousands of people at all levels of business has revealed that there has been no common way to define, talk about, plan, change, or generally deal with others about the many varied aspects of work. It is possible for individuals to talk about *their* work. And when people have a technical language (finance, electronics, manufacturing, etc.), they seem to be able to communicate *about* work. But when we get together to talk about work—what is wrong with it, how to make it better, what needs to change—we find we just don't look at work the same way. This disparity means we do not have the right words to discuss work, or evaluate ways to make it better, because we approach its conceptualization differently.

We begin by exploring a fundamental understanding of work in terms of its dependent elements. This can lead to a highly useful "Work Formula," a model so everyone can always see what's happening in your department.

This is why it is so important to define work—and not just define it, but have a functional "model" to structure, understand, and use daily.

A few months ago a manager wrote asking how to make a significant change in work in his organization. I could have answered him by listing the typical change management approaches that float around the business press today. He could do re-engineering, lean manufacturing, process or flow diagramming, utilize change management, try a quality initiative, and so on. But rather than choosing to reply with one of those, I explained why these approaches concentrate more on the mechanics than on the more important aspect of what work is and how to change it.

Generally, these approaches are also either too time-consuming (wasting time and money) or lack operational ways for individuals and groups to effect the change, meanwhile creating too much angst and lost productivity in the organization. The problem was not that these approaches are intrinsically bad. Rather, each has been shown unoperationalizable by everyone *together*—executive, managers, workers, technical experts, change agents, human resources, and so forth.

This is because we, in business, do not have a common way to define work. If we do not have a way to achieve universal agreement about what presently exists, we cannot envision what *should* exist, nor can we identify the actual problems. We then find that we cannot evaluate the various interventions for change, which means that commitment to the change is also frequently confusing or missing. All these current approaches to work change, improvement, implementation, and management are less than optimally functional or effective. They share a fundamental failure to define what work is, or at a minimum how to best represent and manipulate the actual work of the organization to best meet desired business needs and achieve results.

As a precursor to defining work, we need to recognize that work is a shared process, not just what he, she, you, or I individually do. Therefore work must be defined, committed to, and implemented accordingly, not only up and down your organization, but with suppliers (internal and external) and customers. To do so we need a common way to look at work that allows every point of view and recognizes every required need. That may seem a bit too simple or too daunting, or even too naïve, but we ask that you take our word for it at the moment, try what we suggest in the context of being a manager with your team, and you will begin to see results—big and little.

What Is Work?

The answer to, "What is work?" might seem to be, "It's the activity we engage in," or "What I get paid to do," or "Creating profit." These answers are true, but limited, as we will discover. And each is missing other important elements of the definition of work. We need a way to include everything people might answer when asked what work is.

We begin by asking a series of work-related questions, which will help us to define work completely. Then we can create a template of the parts of work that can be assembled, or populated if you will, to meet various business applications, including that of managing. We will create a paradigm—or more accurately, a formula—of work that can be re-created time and time again and bring clarity to work organization, managing, decisions, and actions.

These are the six questions that will help you arrive at a definition of work in your organization. Answer them for yourself for your own job as a manager, and then answer them for your team as a whole, and for the individual job holders on your team:

1. Does each job holder [and the team] know exactly what deliverables are to be produced?
2. Can they state the "value" or impact these deliverables will have for them, for customers, and for the business as a whole?
3. Can they explicitly identify what will initiate their work and list the resources they need to produce their deliverables?
4. Does each job holder [and the team] know what internal rules and/or external regulations impact how they do the work?
5. Does everyone consistently follow certain steps to achieve the outputs and consequences?
6. Can you and they make mid-course corrections and tell when the work is over?

If you have any doubts about any of the answers—yours or theirs—your team's understanding and execution of its work is in jeopardy, as is your capacity to manage. Furthermore, even the answers to each question would be incomplete if you didn't know the interrelationship of those answers.

We will show you how the answers to these questions form a fundamental, behavioral understanding of work that impacts individuals, teams, and your management of the same. Having clarity on the answers and their cause-and-effect relationship will go a long way toward improving your performance and that of your group. Answering these six questions and connecting the answers introduces a succinct, easy to understand and apply "formula" of work. That formula can lead to an operational understanding of work allowing you to understand and manage effectively and efficiently.

What Are the Elements of Work and How Do They Relate in Terms of Cause and Effect?

1. Does your team and each job holder know exactly what deliverables are to be produced? Do you all describe results in the same way?

We often see bewilderment on the faces of employees, managers, and executives when we ask, "What do you produce?" Someone will finally mention one item and then another; sometimes we have to probe with an additional question, "Who are your clients/customers, and what are the tangible products or services you provide them?" You might think that everyone in the organization could readily spell out what they produce, but if you ask them, you may receive a disparate set of answers.

Why is this question about the output of work so hard to answer? We believe that most people commonly think of work as the activity in which they are engaged. Later we will identify these as the "process steps" of work. Rarely do we think of the end result/the output/the deliverable to our customer, client, or colleague as a key element of our work. Nor do we often think of the recipient of this output—the product or service we deliver. Whatever the reasons for this lack of clarity, a definition of work requires a clear understanding of the outputs (or deliverables) a person or team is expected to produce.

2. Can they state the "value" or impact these deliverables will have for them, for customers, and for the business as a whole?

Knowing why you are doing the work is intrinsically important to achieving both personal goals and business expectations. Can you state explicitly the result your work is to achieve and which outputs contribute to that achievement? The impact of what you produce (value-add) is a part of the definition of work. Why would we do work if it didn't have value to others? We will come to refer to value as "consequences," a behavioral term and one which, in business, should be positive.

3. Can they explicitly identify what will initiate their work and list the resources they need to produce their deliverables?

This may be the easiest question for everyone in the workforce to answer. We have a pretty good idea of what we need to do our work in the way of resources, such as specific data, physical tools, other people, facilities, funds, and so forth. However, one of the more critical inputs to our work is that which begins or "triggers" the work. This includes specific requests, orders, etc., from clients, as well as what a manager requests us to do. Thus, as we shall shortly describe, there are two types of "inputs" to be aware of in your work.

4. Does each job holder and the team know what internal rules and/or external regulations impact how they do the work?

Many workers and managers don't realize how their work is governed or regulated by policies and rules that come from either inside or outside the organization. Perhaps they become aware of them only when they get into trouble for not following them. Some governance for jobs—such as safety regulations—is obvious. Others may not seem so obviously constrained. Company policies on treatment of employees (such as HR law, Fair Labor Standards Act, labor contracts, ethics rules) must be known and adhered to. Success at work requires compliance with all pertinent guidelines. Some organizations provide training on such rules, but others create a landmine for employees and managers to traverse. Upon occasion we have found organizations where all the rules were under lock and key. We call any rules and regulations the "conditions" of work.

5. Does everyone consistently follow certain steps to achieve the outputs and consequences? Do they agree on what they are?

Again, the steps needed to produce an output are generally well known, but may not be so commonly agreed on by workers and managers. They may not understand how their "steps" impact others' work. The questions are: "Are the steps you normally perform understood by people in other parts of the organization?" "Are there circumstances under which changing steps is called for when conditions dictate it?"

In our work modeling, we have seen two extremes when it comes to articulating process: On the one hand, no general procedures exist, so no process maps are available. People do their jobs based on a common assumption about the work; they may have "grown up" in the organization, and therefore seem to understand what is going on. At the other end, we see organizations where every single process is mapped. Both of these extremes share a common problem: The connection between the core process and the process of the job is unclear at best. And when changes are instigated, the changes can create confusion. Process steps need to be defined at a level for practical use, but not so rigidly as to rule out necessary changes.

6. Can you and they make mid-course corrections and tell when the work is over?

No other element of work is more often missing than what we label "feedback." Neither managers nor workers regularly get the level of feedback they need to assure they are doing their job the right way. Most feedback comes in negative terms as a response to failure. Businesses rarely ask for feedback without associated negativism. Even moderate clarification or improvement in the use of certain feedback can lead to marked improvement in job, team, and management performance.

The Interaction or Systemic Feature in a Definition of Work

When you have clear answers to the six questions above, you can begin to explore the second major aspect of defining work: that is, the behavioral interaction of these six elements of work. You need to know this behavioral interaction because it tells you how work happens, and also how to manage changes to it. Since you work with or manage others, knowing the interaction of the work elements allows you to identify what effects changes in any one element can produce in the others as well. You will be better able to identify where the work problems exist, identify how to improve them, and more easily implement strategic or technological work changes. Everyday performance of work will improve dramatically.

In the chapters that follow, we introduce the Work Formula which is one part of the overall Language of Work. The Language of Work formula explored in the rest of this book exists as a specific aid for understanding and managing work.

Chapter 2

A Work Formula for Understanding and Managing Work

To effectively organize and manage, we need to have a common, shared understanding of what really comprises work. We need to agree on which elements truly help everyone understand the work, and how those elements relate to one another behaviorally. Without such agreement, we invariably end up with many personal opinions that prevent us from coming to consensus about the simplest aspects of work, much less the more complex: how to organize, implement, and manage work.

We introduce a systemic Work Formula to help you understand, organize, and manage your department. Everyone will share the Work Formula to unify their understanding and execution of work.

For example, one person says that work is defined as "winning proposals" (which is a consequence) and another says it is defined by "the customer" (who is important, but an input and the ultimate receiver). A third says work is "hard," which is a descriptor, but not a definer. Each person will fiercely support their position, often leading to misunderstandings, conflict, and lack of consensus, fragmented commitment, and needed improvements. By agreeing that the *definition* of work must include all the elements we introduced in Chapter 1, we can achieve shared clarity on any given piece of work. Put another way, if you think work is composed of two elements, I think it has six elements, and someone else thinks there are three, we are in trouble from the get-go. Only when we agree to a common work language and use it together can we begin to systematically organize, support, and manage the work. We also find that having a common language allows people to think in new ways and build on each other's best thinking.

The six questions posed in the previous chapter led us to a formula we refer to as a "Work Formula," the anchor of The Language of Work. Just as an architect's model represents what a house or building will eventually be, our Work Formula represents operationally what work is. For example, once populated with the data of your particular work at the job and team level, it shows a clear picture that all parties created and can agree to. Once we agree upon the data in this Work Formula, we are in a position to apply it to critical business models. The clarity that is created by applying the Work Formula to various levels and layers of business will make it possible to assure alignment, create transparency, and help make continuous improvements to all aspects of what it takes to be a successful organization.

The Language of Work: Six-Element Work Formula

The Language of Work employs the Work Formula of six related and systemic elements that we believe define and operationalize work. You could almost think of it as a "template" for work. In the same way that anyone can now produce a professional presentation given a PowerPoint template, so too can you now fill the six-element Work Formula and understand any kind of work—current or future. In this way organizations can capture the essence of work and apply this to needed business applications. By doing so, we keep it sweet and simple for everyone—without losing anything that is essential.

To summarize and set the stage for postulating a Work Formula, the six questions concerning what is work in Chapter 1 are now posted here again, to which we attach a short one- or two-word label:

Do You Know What Work Is?

ELEMENT	QUESTION
Outputs	Does your team and each job holder know exactly what deliverables are expected to be produced? Do you all describe results in the same way?
Inputs	Can they explicitly identify what will initiate their work and list the resources they need to produce their deliverables?
Conditions	Does each job holder and the team know what internal rules and/or external regulations impact how they do the work?
Consequences	Can they state the "value" or impact these deliverables will have for them, for customers and the business they are a part of?
Process Steps	Does everyone consistently follow certain steps to achieve the outputs and consequences,, and do they agree on what they are?
Feedback	Can you and they make mid-course corrections and tell when the work is over?

Figure 1

These six key work elements are now shown in Figure 2 in the form of a flow diagram. The diagram is important because it affords a way to depict the interrelationships of the six elements. We need to elaborate on what these elements mean and their relationship to one another so that we are all thinking of them in the same way and in the context of the business in order to have a shared meaning when defining and deciding how to organize, manage, implement, or change work without confusion or misunderstanding.

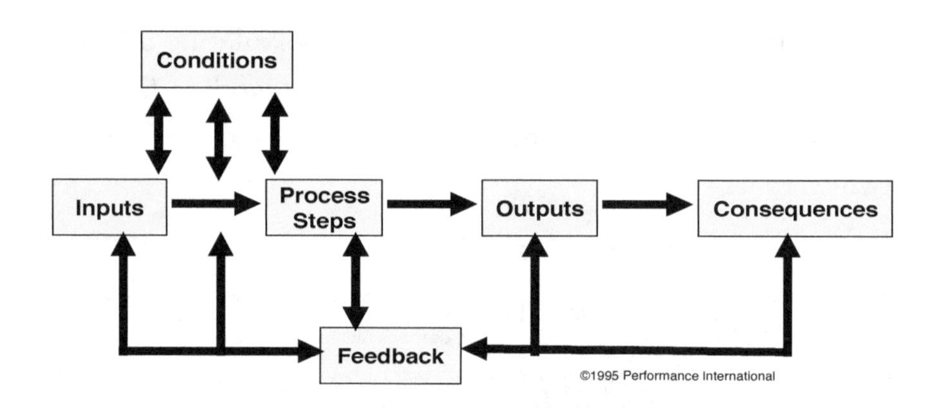

Figure 2

In our consultation with enterprises to better define, align, organize, improve, and implement their work, we use an introductory Language of Work (LoW) tool entitled the "The Work Formula: A 10-Minute Teach." It is a short, convenient, and effective orientation to each of the six elements of work using an analogy drawn from American football. Here we use a limited version of the 10-Minute Teach; the full version can be found as a YouTube presentation at https://youtu.be/Nn7tLm4nRLU.

Imagine that we are ready to begin modeling the work of your department. As the facilitator of this session, we say:

"The Language of Work Formula is a way to represent the interrelated elements that make up work. The Work Formula can be used to define work at various levels and layers of a business. Today we are going to put together your work group (or job) model. As you look at the Work Formula (in Figure 2) each of you will recognize every word and give it your own personal meaning. However, we need to establish and share a ***common*** *meaning for each word. These six words also have a dynamic relation to one another, which we illustrate by the arrows, and the relationships need to be well understood and applied individually and collectively. We will look at the definitions first, and then the behavioral relationships.*

You will note that three of the words—inputs, process steps, and output—are the classic manufacturing model. Henry Ford, for example, understood and applied this model quite effectively in building an entire industry based on producing automobiles. He took various identified resources (inputs), utilized them through assembly-line manufacturing (process steps) to produce outputs (cars). That was all he was concerned with as far as an understanding of work back then. It was ground-breaking at the time in the definition of work and had significant world-wide consequences. But Ford's view of work assumed that the workers were cogs in a machine. Now we know that humans are not robots and need data to perform well. Recognizing that performance is the behavior of people, we have added three additional words that capture work. These additional words are: consequences, conditions, and feedback. Thus, when outputs are produced, they must result in usable ***consequences*** *to the business, follow important* ***conditions*** *that govern the work, and are aided by* ***feedback*** *(communication) that helps do the work correctly and to the satisfaction of clients or customers.*

A sports analogy, American football, will tie these work elements together and give further clarity in the use of the six elements that comprise work. In this instance, let's take the work execution of one work group in football, the defense, and model it using the Work Formula. Defense is the work group that tries to keep the other team's offense from scoring. We will illustrate this in a very basic model without the usual details of a real work group model (to be shown later). The defense work group model is shown in Figure 3.

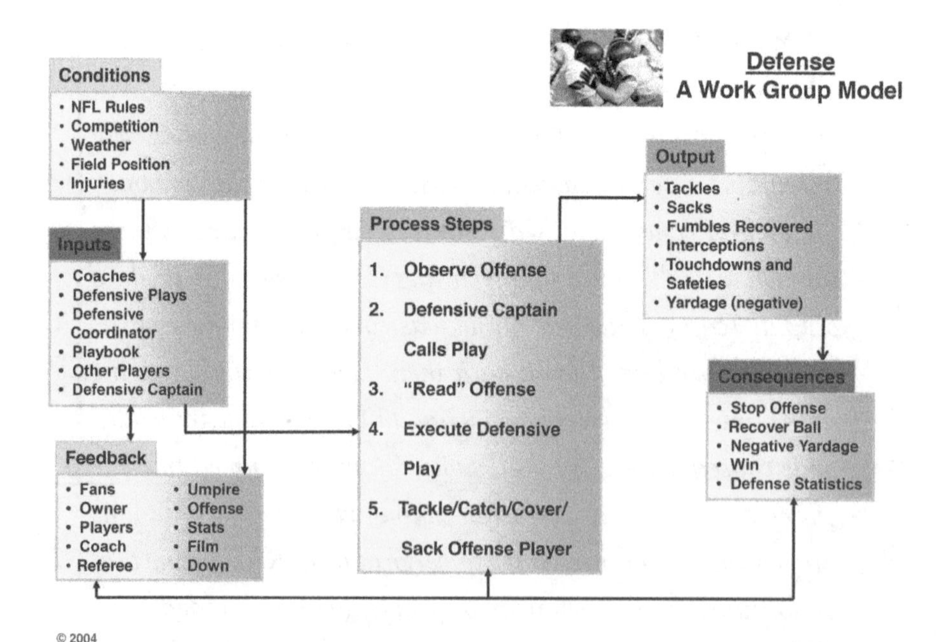

Figure 3

When a work group such as this is modeled, we begin by specifying the outputs (listed at the right). This tells us what the group produces as products or services. For example, the defense (work group) tackles, sacks, recovers fumbles, and tries to intercept the ball and so on. It does this to achieve the consequences of countering the efforts of the opposing team's offense. To do this, it needs certain inputs from the coaches, other players, the defensive coordinator, and so on. It must follow certain conditions such as the NFL Rules, its own defensive playbook, etc. It achieves the outputs by using prescribed process steps that we have generalized here at a very high level in a five-step sequence—understanding, of course, that more detailed steps would be specified as to how each output is achieved. And the work of the defense is enhanced and encouraged by the use of feedback from such sources as the umpire, fans, and other players. Again, greater detail will be provided in our actual work group model.

This just illustrates one level of work in an organization—the work group level. Continuing our analogy, other levels would be the business unit (franchise), the core processes (play of the game, marketing, merchandizing, recruiting, etc.), and jobs (players). In organizing and managing your department, we are concerned with modeling only work groups and jobs. (Note: for managers of more than one department, you will need to also model core processes as well. This is delineated in the Business Model of the Language of Work Trilogy.*)*

We have seen a work group modeled, so let's look at an individual job. We will define it again at a high level, for illustrative purposes.

Figure 4 illustrates the job model of a quarterback, one of several players on a football team. Using the Work Formula six-element template, we can model the quarterback job in the same way we did the work group. By doing this, for the first time the relationship between the team's work groups (defense, offense, and special teams) and the work of various individual job holders can be made visible, which allows us to align the individual jobs to the work group and vice versa. As you see here, you can illustrate the quarterback job in terms of the outputs produced to achieve consequences by using certain inputs, following conditions, process steps, and aided by feedback.

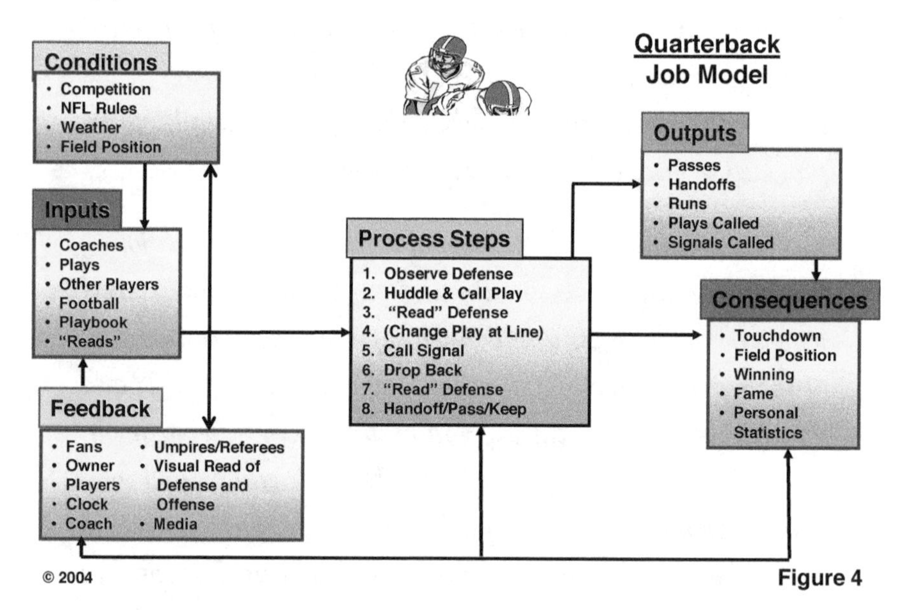

Figure 4

Figure 5 provides a useful summary of the six elements that comprise the LoW Formula. These elements are listed, defined, and typified in the order in which all levels of work would be best modeled. You can keep this in front of you as we begin to model our department and your job.

(END of 10-Minute Teach Narrative)

The Language of Work Formula

Work Modeling Definition Job Aid

ELEMENT	DEFINITION	TYPICAL SOURCES	TYPES
Output	That which is produced/ provided for stakeholders as tangible deliverables	• Services • Products • Knowledge	
Input	The resources and requests available or needed to produce outputs. What must be present for something (the output) to happen.	• Client Needs • People • Ideas • Equipment • Facilities • Funds • Information • Specific requests	➢ Triggers ➢ Resources
Conditions	Existing factors that influence the use of inputs and processes to produce outputs.	• Rules • Policies • Regulations • Governance	➢ Internal ➢ External
Consequences	The effects that an output has on a person, product, service, or situation.	• Customer Satisfaction • Needs Met • Problem Solved • Opportunity Realized	➢ Company ➢ Stakeholders ➢ Personal ➢ Societal
Process Steps	The steps completed to use the inputs, under the conditions, in order to produce the outputs.	Steps are represented by action verbs such as: • Produce • Review • Edit • etc.	
Feedback	That which completes the work cycle; response to outputs that confirms success or indicates adjustment is needed. Also, response to processing, conditions, and feedback.	• Client Reactions • Information Needs • Reinforcements	➢ During ➢ After

Figure 5

You will find that this way of defining work is a straightforward, objective depiction of work results (outputs and consequences) and describes how the work is executed (inputs, conditions, process steps, and feedback) to produce the results. We have found that members of an organization intuitively know all these aspects of work, but have not had a template to use in defining and agreeing on such a useful form for analysis, organization, and improvement. Thus, the Work Formula provides a common framework for understanding not only know what is currently going on (the AS IS state), but also for planning (the TO BE state).

Based on this, we can now explain how to specifically define and manage your department.

Chapter 3

Work Analytics for the Managing Model

Tools for Defining and Implementing the Managing Model

The authors have devised a set of ways (tools) to actualize the Work Formula for defining and implementing the Business Model, Managing Model, and Working Model. These Work Analytic Tools (WATs), as we refer to them, make applying the Work Formula easy to use in defining, implementing, and measuring work to meet business needs. These tools include such things as work models, matrices, the Work Formula itself, and other tools that you will be introduced to. Each will be explained and illustrated relative to the three work implementation models of the LoW. Here, relative to the Managing Model, we introduce the Work Formula itself as an analytic tool. In addition, you will learn how to use Work Group Model and the Job Model as key analytic tools for work execution. Finally, the Work Support Matrix as a Work Analytic Tool will be introduced to assure work support.

This chapter introduces a set of analytical tools that can be used to analyze, implement, and continuously improve the Managing Model.

The Work Formula

The Work Formula, Figure 6, is not just a means for modeling various levels of work execution and representing the layers of work support, but also is a way to actualize work—in this instance many of the various management functions such as work planning, work orientation, deciding training needs, performance reviews, and the like.

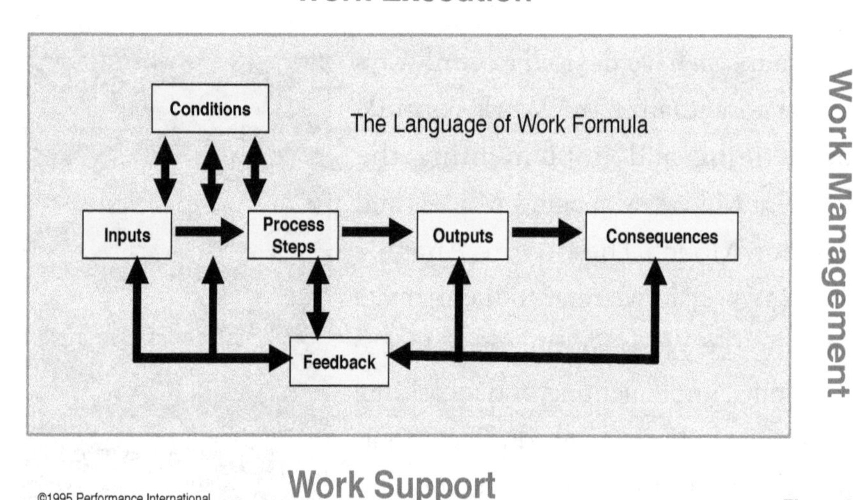

Figure 6

Work Models

There are four basic kinds of work models; each one reflecting a different work execution level:

- Business Unit Model
- Core Processes Models
- Job Models
- Work Group Models

With some exception, each uses the format shown in Figures 7 and 8 to capture inputs, process steps, outputs, conditions, consequences, and feedback.

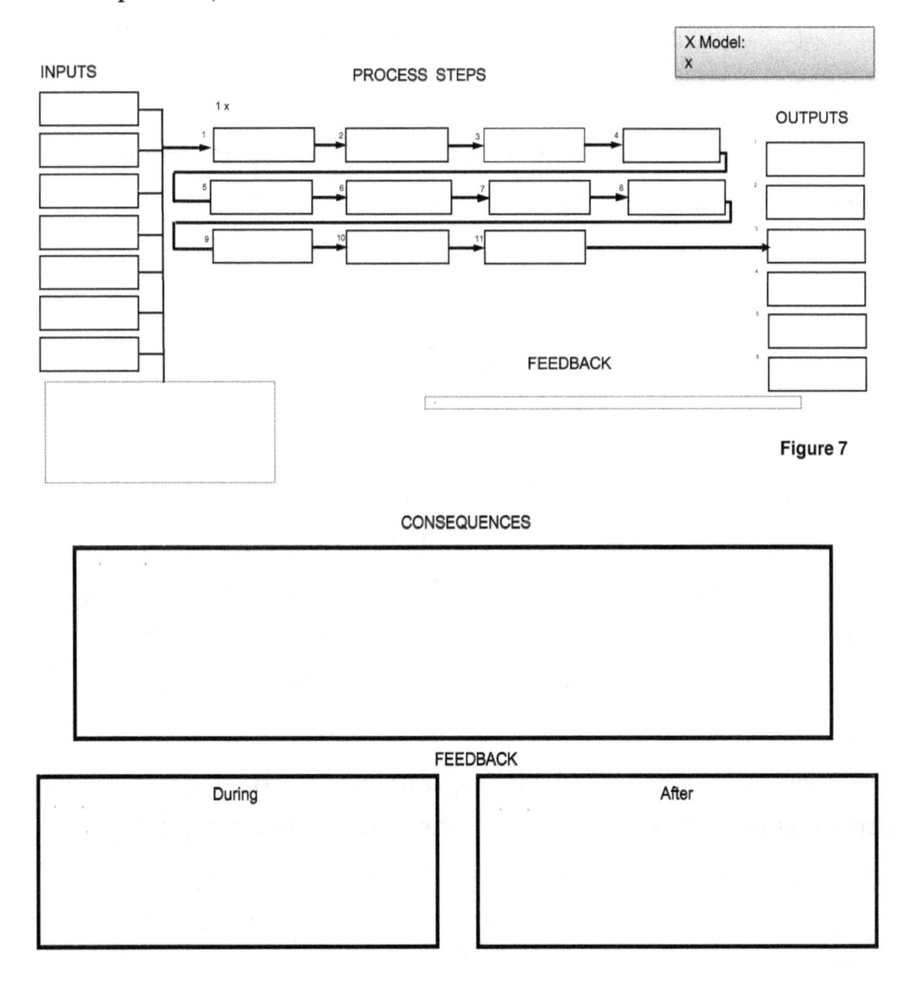

Figure 7

Figure 8

Work models are a specialized LoW version of flowcharting that incorporate all six elements of the Work Formula. Not only do the work models help portray what work is to be achieved and how at each level, but they also show the relationship—alignment—to each other. This alignment helps achieve overall work efficiency and effectiveness.

Models may be represented in either a state of TO BE, AS IS, or both, as needed. If desired, they may also be used to achieve a level of work transparency never before realized.

Regarding to the Managing Model, you will learn to use both Work Group Models and Job Models as they relate to your role in facilitating work.

Work Matrices

Work matrices are used to display the layers of work that an organization must assure are in place to support work execution. These matrices relate to work standards, work support (see Figure 9), human relations, and financial support. Each matrix employs the work formula on one axis within the context of the four levels of work execution. These matrices may be used to both decide what work layer support is desired, as well as help in the continuous evaluation of their merit on an ongoing basis, helping to determine what work support needs improving. We recommend that you tailor the matrices to your specific business environment.

WORK SUPPORT MATRIX

	INPUT	CONDITIONS	PROCESS	OUTPUT	CONSEQUENCES	FEEDBACK
BUSINESS UNIT	*STRATEGY & BUS. PLANS* 1A	*CULTURE / CONTROLS* 1B	*ADMINISTRATIVE SYSTEMS* 1C	*BUSINESS DELIVERABLES* 1D	*BUSINESS RESULTS* 1E	*BUSINESS MEASUREM./EVALUAT.* 1F
CORE PROCESSES	*PROCESS RESOURCES* 2A	*REGULATIONS/ POLICIES* 2B	*TECHNOLOGIES (SOFT & HARD)* 2C	*PROCESS DELIVERABLES* 2D	*PROCESS RESULTS* 2E	*CONFIRMATIONS & CORRECTIONS* 2F
JOBS	*CLIENT NEEDS & RESOURCES* 3A	*WORK INFLUENCES* 3B	*WORK METHODS* 3C	*JOB DELIVERABLES* 3D	*INDIVIDUAL RESULTS* 3E	*CONFIRMATIONS & SELF ADJUSTMENT* 3F
WORK GROUPS	*CLIENT NEEDS & RESOURCES* 4A	*VALUES & PRACTICES* 4B	*INTERFACE/ RELATIONSHIPS* 4C	*WORK GROUP DELIVERABLES* 4D	*WORK GROUP RESULTS* 4E	*MANAGEMENT/TEAM INFORMATION SYSTEM* 4F

Figure 9

For the Managing Model, we will specifically look at how to use a Work Matrix for assuring adequate Work Support.

In addition, throughout *The Work Trilogy* you will find a range of other Work Analytic Tools that are used to operationalize the Work Formula for executives, managers, and workers including the following:

- AS IS/TO Be Models and Tables
- Dots On Models
- Work Plan
- Jobs Identified to Processes
- Work Analysis Aid
- Cultural Audit
- Worker Verbatims
- Etc.

Chapter 4

Overview of Understanding and Managing Work

There are more than fifty ways that the Work Formula can be applied in businesses/organizations. We refer to these collectively as the three Work Implementation Models, as well as the various ways the Language of Work can be applied to organizational effectiveness. A list of these ways is to be found at the very end of the book, but for now, we are concerned only with applying the Work Formula to your role as the manager.

> The Work Formula can be applied to a great variety of business needs. For you, as a manager, we delineate various roles to which you will want to apply the Work Formula in different ways.

As illustrated in Figure 10, below, we are going to be looking at three broad managerial functions you as a manager are responsible for: work execution, work support, and work management. The first two will help you gain a fuller understanding of work while the last will demonstrate how to manage work. Each is significant in and of itself, but they relate to one another, and can be approached in common using the Work Formula, which will allow you to align and integrate the three roles, rather than approach what are seemingly separate, unrelated functions. Here we provide a brief introduction and show the relationship of these management functions as a prelude to illustrating each in more detail in the chapters that follow.

Work Execution

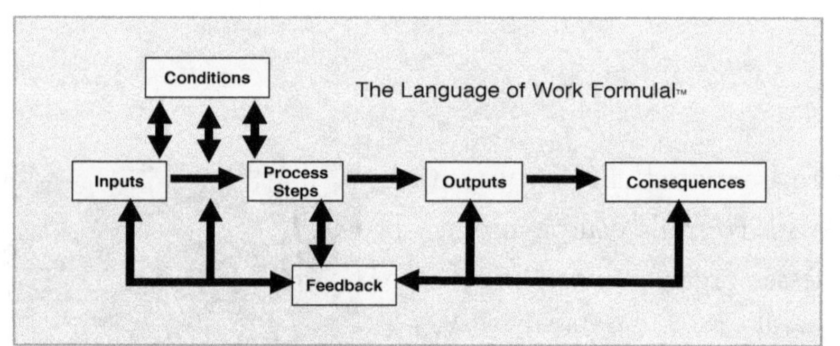

Work Management

 Work Support **Figure 10**

Work Execution (Chapter 5)

Work execution, as the title suggests, means doing the work. This occurs at different levels in an enterprise—namely, the business unit, core processes, job groups, and work groups. Since in this book we are concerned with a single manager and his/her team, we confine work execution to the most common and basic form of management. Thus, we will not deal with a management style involving accountability for several teams across core processes, although the principles will be similar. A basic team effort necessitates the modeling of only the single work group and the job models that fall within that work group. Both work group and jobs will be approached from a profound understanding of what work is between manager and workers.

Using the Work Formula will allow you and your workers to properly link (or align) your work collectively and individually. We will demonstrate that this concept of alignment is critical, so that each level of work is congruent with the others. And, just as importantly it will allow a form a work transparency beyond anything you may have thought possible before. One comes to understand more fully not only his or her individual work, but that of others, the team, and to some degree the entire enterprise.

Work Support (Chapter 6)

Jobs do not exist in a vacuum. Rather, the performance of jobs requires a number of resources that enhance the likelihood of successful work execution. These interventions include a variety of means, resources, initiatives, programs, and the like that the business needs and should provide. It's convenient and useful to simply call them "interventions," since they all are intended to be ways of supporting work execution. For example, a water ballet team needs a coach, optimal water conditions, proper attire, and the like to do their best work. So too does your group and individual work execution require support in several forms.

For example, it should be obvious that certain skills and knowledge are needed for one to execute work. Therefore, the organization provides support in the form of a hiring function that finds skilled and experienced workers, a method to evaluate performance so that work can be improved, and training courses, among many other interventions. Some of these Work Support initiatives and resources are under your control or influence; others come from and under the influence of senior management and their own support personnel. What the Language of Work provides is a tool to identify and analyze the work support needs so you and your work force can offer input as to their quality and utility. Those interventions not under your control will also be assessed by you and your work force so that you can influence intervention improvement by demonstrating how work support does or does not impact work execution. For example, if you find that the current performance review process is not working for you and your staff, you can easily determine this and ask that it be improved. Or, you will learn how to improve performance reviews yourself using the Work Formula, as well many other management functions you normally perform in your daily routine.

Work support is a way to ensure that one has the "healthy" work environment needed to assure efficient and effective work execution. Enterprises need to constantly evaluate the effectiveness of the various aspects of work support by tying the work support interventions and resources directly to their impact on work execution. The Work Formula makes this possible by aligning work execution and work support.

Work Management (Chapter 7)

There is a great deal of information available on managing work, as we stated in Chapter 1. Here we are going to take a different approach. Since you will be learning a viable Work Formula for defining and organizing work execution, along with the assortment of ways to support that work to assure a healthy work culture, we will show you how to use that same Work Formula to facilitate/ manage the work.

Chapter 5

Work Execution: Defining Your Department Using the Language of Work Formula

> The Language of Work can be used to organize and align your department for work execution. This is done in the form of a work group model to which jobs are linked, followed by defining job models for everyone who works in your department.

Figures 11 and 12 represent a sample department, illustrating how to populate the Work Formula graphically to show work group execution. At first glance, it may seem like just another flow diagram, but it is significantly different. This one represents the full picture of what constitutes work execution.

A Sample Work Group Model

The sample department, an IT function, is from a real engagement the authors completed with a client. We won't show the entire work group model. Rather, we illustrate one page of sample process steps, inputs, outputs, and conditions, and a second page of consequences and feedback. A complete work group model would average five to seven pages, and it is not needed for our purposes here. With an experienced facilitator, a typical work group model can be completed in four to six hours.

In Figure 11 you see the specification for four of the six elements of a work group model:

- Outputs (on the right)
- Inputs (on the left)
- Conditions (at the bottom), and
- Process Steps in the center.

Figure 12 shows the Consequences and Feedback, the other two elements of the Work Formula for a typical work model.

Most departments have five to seven major outputs. These are the products or services provided/delivered to its internal or external customers/clients. Our sample work group, IT Support Services, produces the nine services shown in the following list. We shall deal more closely with outputs 4 and 5 for illustrative purposes. You find these two outputs on the right side of the work group model (Figure 11).

1. Problems Solved
2. Operations Recovery Planned
3. Data Center Services Provided
4. Department-wide Security Provided
5. Developmental Life Cycle Planned
6. Research/Advice Consulting Provided
7. IT Assets Managed
8. Data Managed
9. IT Audits Conducted

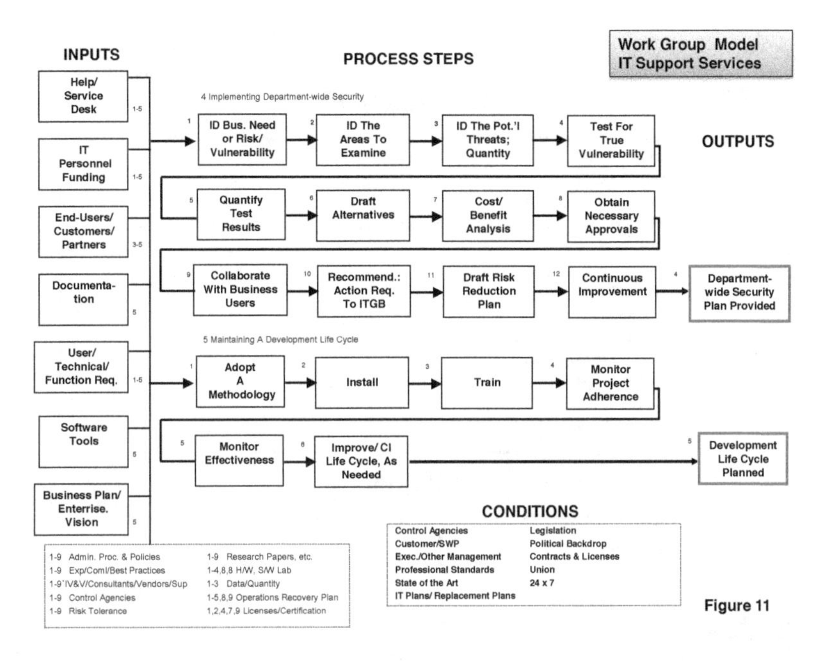

Figure 11

Looking further at Figure 11, you can see that in order to produce these outputs, the group will need certain inputs, both triggers that initiate the work and resources needed to carry it out. The help desk, for example, is a typical trigger input, while software tools are a typical resource input. There is no order of importance to the inputs, but rather the range of needed inputs by the work group in question. Each has a separate box and is cross-referenced to the outputs they help produce.

At the bottom of Figure 11 is an extensive list of rules and regulations, or what we call conditions (governances) that the group must be aware of and follow. Contracts and licenses, for example, are one kind of condition.

Next Figure 11 shows two sets of process steps, one each for the two outputs illustrated. Output 4 has a 12-step process and output 5 has 6 steps.

Work Group Model
IT Support Services

CONSEQUENCES

1. Increased efficiency (outputs 1-9)
2. Customer satisfaction (outputs 1-9)
3. Cost/appropriate (Balanced Score Card) (outputs 1-9)
4. Stability and consistency of department-wide processes (outputs 1-9)
5. Standardization (outputs 1-9)
6. Trust of process and output (outputs 1-9)
7. Acceptance of expertise (outputs 1-9)
8. Happier employees (outputs 1-4,6,8)
9. Improved/informed decision making (outputs 2, 6-9)
10. Accountability by all parties (outputs 1,2,4,5,7,8)
11. Improved resource management (outputs 1-9)
12. Support the accomplishment of DWR Mission & Vision (outputs 1-9)
13. Appropriate security of IT environment (outputs 2-4,6,8-9)

FEEDBACK

During

1. Client
2. Management
3. IT Governance
4. Performance Monitoring SW
5. Peers
6. Vendors
7. Professional Societies

After

1. Client
2. Management
3. IT Governance
4. Control Agencies
5. Audit
6. Security Performance
7. Performance Monitoring SW
8. Peers
9. Vendors
10. Professional Societies

Figure 12

Figure 12 lists first the positive consequences that are to be achieved by the sample department. Each statement is a value outcome to be attained as a result of a set of outputs. For example, the first consequence, "Increased efficiency," is the result of all department outputs, while consequence 13, "Appropriate security of IT environment," is the result of outputs 2-4, 6, and 8-9.

Taken together, this work group model is a graphic representation of how the work will be executed. It establishes consensus by members of the work group and a unified commitment to the nature of the work. In the future, it becomes the basis upon which change will be planned and aligned to need improvements or perhaps new products and services, or technology innovations. It also represents what you will manage/facilitate in your role as the group manager/leader.

Naming Jobs Needed To Execute the Work

With a work group model in hand, we suggest that you next identify the jobs that are needed (current or future) to execute the work. This step is crucial to making work execution seamless: You want to align jobs to the work group. Until now, this has generally been a gut or guess process, which sounds great, but which is not easily or dependably successful. But with the Work Formula, it is possible to precisely align the jobs to the work group.

We need a way to "align" the jobs to the work group so that they are congruent. In other words, whatever the individual worker/job is, it should match the group effort, and vice versa. We all know what happens when people work at odds with group effort. If an individual pays little attention to consequences, to following the rules, or to delays in process steps, this affects what the group achieves in either effectiveness or efficiency or both.

Alignment can be represented in the following Work Execution Alignment diagram. You will note that the six-element Work Formula is the centerpiece used to link work alignment by assuring the congruence between the outputs of the work group and those of the individual, as well as the other five elements of work. Thus, each worker will use those elements of work from the work group as they apply to their jobs. It's a good way to cross-check that all the work is covered, related to each job, and avoids duplication of effort. Where differences in responsibility and conflicts occur, they can be addressed using the work group and job models to keep everyone centered on the efficient and effective execution of the work.

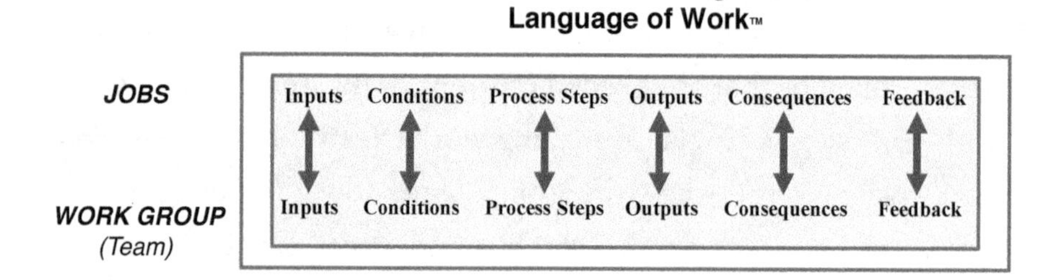

Note: There are other aspects of work alignment involving things like work support, standards, and the like. We will introduce some of this in the next two chapters, and they are explained more extensively in other writings by the authors of *The Work Trilogy*.

Specifically, how do we assure this alignment when modeling the work? It has two parts to it:

1. Identifying the jobs to the work group, and
2. Modeling the jobs.

The innovative approach to identifying jobs that we will describe and illustrate will clarify for everyone who does what and how it links to others inside and outside your department. This is a very easy and powerful step in organizing your department.

In Figure 13, below, you see again the IT Work Group Model. This time, however, in this Work Analytic Tool (jobs named to process steps), it has been color-coded. The question to pose at each process step is, "Who does this work?" At the top of the sample IT Work Group Model, we have identified four different jobs in this sample work group that exist to execute the work. In step 1 of output 4, "Department-Wide Security Plan Developed," there are three different jobs that perform all or part of this one step. Two jobs will be involved in steps 2 and 3, while step 4 involves only one job. This color-coding of jobs to work group process steps thus creates a picture of who does the work and how that work relates to other jobs.

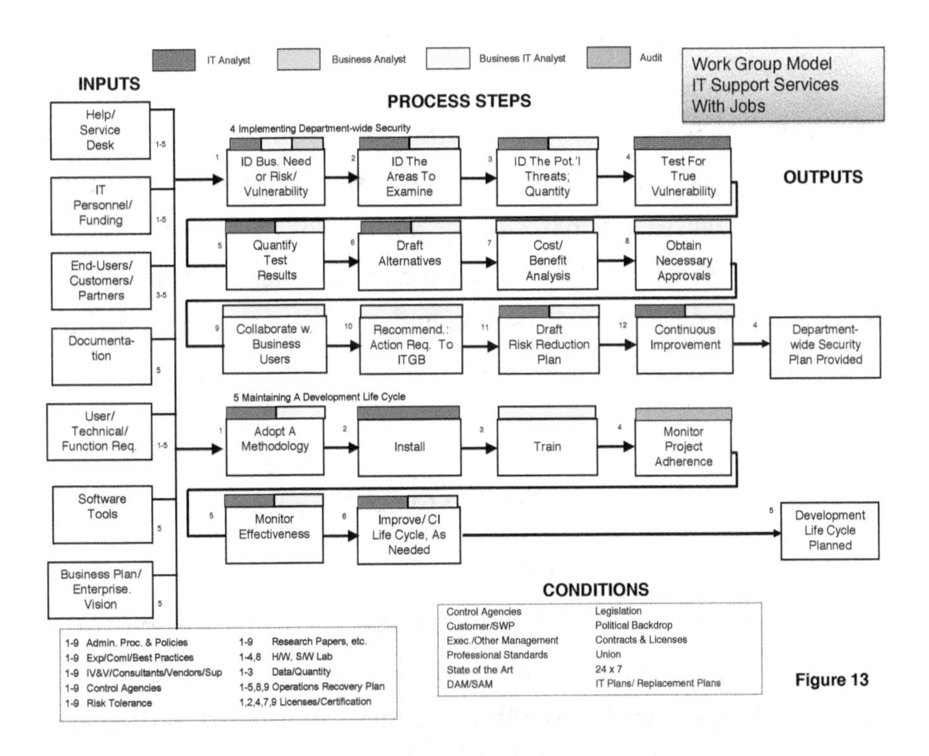

Figure 13

Identifying jobs in this manner is a key to developing an aligned, performance-centric organization: Each individual knows what he or she is to accomplish, as well how each step is related to his or her own and others' work. You can use current job titles to identify jobs or, if you desire, you could use job titles that are either more generic (Clerk 1, 2, 3) or creatively titled, such as "Hunter," "Gatherer," "Analyzer." Guidance on this is provided by the authors in their other online and print resources.

Because jobs are now clearly operational and tied to the group work to be accomplished, it is then possible to look at the number of people needed to accomplish each deliverable. This is best done at the job level, but even at the work group level, one can estimate the number of hours needed to produce each output. This provides a logical and data-based way to determine the number of employees needed to achieve the work group's results. Recent focus on the "bottom line" has allowed management and executives to make unrealistic estimates of the amount of work required. The Language of Work method allows for much finer calibration, and for discussion with executives. Loading of jobs, or determining how many people are needed for each job, could also be accomplished at this point.

Model Each Job

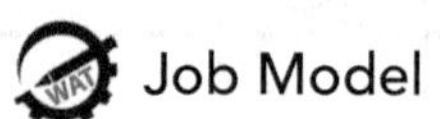

Now that we know what jobs are required to accomplish the work of the group, you can model these jobs. Job Modeling, a Work Analytic Tool of Work Models, is a Language of Work process for delineating exactly how individuals will execute their work in keeping with the team/department work needs made explicit in the Work Group Model. Job modeling uses the same six-element Work Model that was used to model the work group. Job modeling in this form aligns individual work to the purpose and process of the department. Using a common definition of work between work group and jobs builds this alignment.

Modeling jobs is a very efficient, dynamic, and enlightening process. It generally takes about four hours to model almost any job. It requires three to five exemplary job performers (although it can be done with as few as two great job holders). Their only preparation is to bring their experience in the job and awareness of the skills and knowledge required. Exemplary performers can be readily identified by you as the manager. If you are new to the unit, just ask around. Everyone recognizes high-quality performance.

Job Models are a more succinctly defined and useful form of a job description; they show operationally how the work is to be accomplished. Figures 14-17 show a typical Job Model (although we have shown only a sample of various pages of a complete Job Model).

In Figures 14 and 15, you see that a Job (a Business Analyst Model) is represented the same way as was the Work Group Model. Thus, in Figure 14 you find outputs of the job on the right, inputs on the left, conditions at the bottom, and process steps linking inputs and outputs in the middle. You and the workers can "read" this model and see that the job holders initiate their work by certain "trigger" inputs and resources, attend to certain understood conditions, and move through a series of process steps to achieve specific outputs. Figure 15 lists the consequences and feedback. The six elements of work are the foundation of a well-conceived Job Model, but there are other work-related requirements of

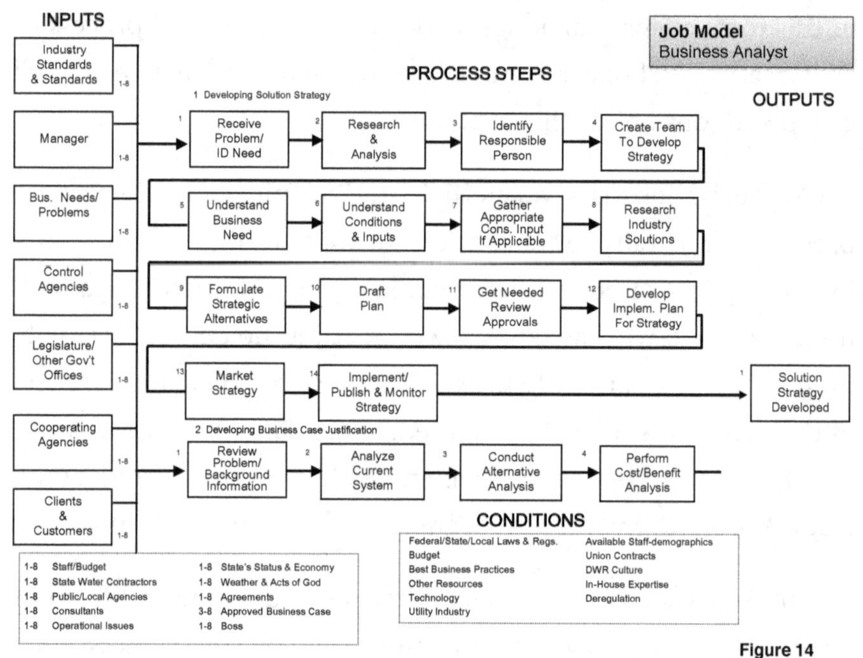

Figure 14

Job Model
Business Analyst

CONSEQUENCES

1. Contributing to viability of Water Resources Agency (outputs 1-8)
2. Integrated system (outputs 1-8)
3. Satisfied customers (outputs 1-8)
4. Cost effectiveness (outputs 1-8)
5. Increased effectiveness and efficiency of IT (outputs 1-8)
6. Changed paradigm (outputs 1-8)
7. Problems solved (outputs 1-8)
8. Informed/skilled users (outputs 3-4)
9. Process improvements (outputs 1-8)
10. Automation of processes (outputs 1-8)
11. Supporting compliance of laws (outputs 1-8)
12. Increased decision support (outputs 1-8)

FEEDBACK

During

1. External Customers
2. System Tools
3. Control Agencies
4. User/Clients
5. Process Owners
6. Executive Management
7. System Performance
8. Vendors
9. Consultants
10. Other Integrated Functional Areas
11. Peers

After

1. Public/Media
2. System Tools
3. Control Agencies
4. User/Clients
5. Process Owners
6. Executive Management
7. System Performance
8. Vendors
9. Consultants
10. Peers
11. External Customers

Figure 15

Job Model
Business Analyst

SKILLS AND KNOWLEDGE

PROCESS

Process for Output 1: Solution Strategy
Skills
- Analytic skills
- Strategic Development
- Planning
- Marketing

Knowledge
- Policies
- Control Agencies
- Public Needs
- IT Industry
- Networking with Peers & Mentors
- Organization Knowledge
- Organization Savvy
- Organization Culture
- Budgeting
- Best Practices
- Business Discipline
- Agency Mission, Goals, Objectives

Process for Output # 2: Business Case Justification
Skills
- Math
- Project Management
- IT Tools/Systems
- Budget

Knowledge
- Applications Limitations
- Agency IT Methodologies

Process for Output # 3: Expertise & Advice
Skills
- Communication: Oral, Written, Verbal, Listening
- Consulting

Knowledge
- Business Disciplines
- Agency Business Processes

Process for Output # 4: Training
Skills
- Training Methods
- Instructional Development
- Analysis
- Evaluation
- Writing

Knowledge
- Business Content

Process for Output # 5: Functional Specifications
Skills
- Research
- Graphics Design

Knowledge
- Application Limitations
- Agency IT Methodologies

Process for Output # 6: Applications/Interfaces/Transactions
Skills
- Analytic
- Writing
- Presentation/Training
- Communication: Interpersonal, Oral, Written

Figure 16

Job Model
Business Analyst

SKILLS AND KNOWLEDGE & ATTRIBUTES

INPUTS

Skills
- Interpreting System Requirements
- Interpreting Data
- Tapping Organization Memory
- Interpersonal Skills
- Reading Implications
- Research & Analysis
- Critical Thinking

Knowledge
- Communication Channels
- Best Practices
- Budgeting
- Organization Culture
- Organization Savvy
- Organization Knowledge
- Policies
- Control Agencies
- Public Needs
- IT Industry
- Networking with Peers & Mentors

FEEDBACK

Skills
- Interpersonal Data
- Interpreting System Requirements

Knowledge
- Communication Channels

CONDITIONS

Skills
- Tapping Organization Memory

Knowledge
- Organization Knowledge
- Organization Savvy
- Organization Culture
- Budgeting
- Best Practices

ATTRIBUTES

- Advocate
- Advisor
- Think Strategically
- Challenge mental ruts
- Practical
- Resourceful
- Make good guesses
- Tenacious
- Impartial
- People Person
- Problem Solver
- Negotiator

Figure 17

individual work that are helpful to include as well, to aid you in your management role. Sometimes these other requirements are mandated by the Human Resources Department. For example, knowing the attributes that exemplary performers need for the job can help you identify and hire people whose natural abilities enhance their successful execution of the work. This is particularly important with knowledge workers whose natural propensities can be difficult to identify.

One of the most common other things to include in a Job Model is illustrated in Figures 16 and 17. This is a Work Analytic Tool mapping Skills and Knowledge to Job Models. These are the skills and knowledge needed to actualize the:

1. Process Steps
2. Inputs
3. Conditions
4. Feedback

We identify skills and knowledge for only these four work elements because these are the elements that produce the outputs and consequences. Workers will need to have or be trained in these skills in order to execute the work. This is, by the way, valuable information for your HR personnel, if you have such a department, for helping find the right people, evaluating their current performance, identifying and providing training, and so forth. The following is a brief description of these and additional add-ons to a typical Job Model that you will want to consider including in all Job Models for your department.

Skills and Knowledge

- Skills are the learned capacity to successfully perform a task with a specified outcome.
- Knowledge is the underlying information or understanding needed to perform a task successfully.

Job Attributes

- Demonstrated cognitive or physical capacities to successfully perform a task with a wide range of possible outcomes.

Job Competencies

- A competency is a measurable human capability required for effective performance.
- Statements that combine outputs with their related consequences are job competencies, while statements based on skills and knowledge are enabling competencies. [Langdon and Whiteside (2004) is an excellent pioneering article available on this subject.]

Entry-Level Skills

- That which the individuals should bring to the job as a minimum requirement to do the job as presently defined.

Accountabilities/Responsibilities

- Statements that capture the chief outcomes the job will be accountable for. Based on Job Models, they can be a combination of the outputs and consequences for each position, similar in scope to competencies.

By way of a summary, you can see that a Job Model is a dynamic, clear picture of what is to be done as work by a person and how. When aligned to the Work Group Model, it helps assure that what the individual does is congruent with what the group is doing collectively. As we transition from our discussion of work execution to other considerations related to work support and work management, two questions are to be considered:

1. Can you identify what the organization does well—or could do better—to support the execution of your department's work and that of the job holders?
2. How does the manager facilitate getting the best work from the team?

We will see how the Work Formula can be used to answer these questions.

Chapter 6

Work Support: Assuring a Healthy Work Environment

The work group and job models specify how the work is to be done in order to achieve your department's function. But other requirements influencing work must also be well-defined, installed, attended to, or improved upon because they truly impact getting the work done.

Work involves more than work execution. How should the business support the work to assure a healthy environment? What is your role as the manager in ensuring work support?

As an old friend and colleague, Geary Rummler (1990) once noted, "... if you pit a good performer against a bad system, the system will win every time."

The LoW use of the terminology "Work Support" is similar to what is generally referred to as "culture." Some authors (see Carlton and Lineberry, 2004) have coined the term "cultural due diligence" to indicate the need to constantly audit and assure that the culture supports getting the work done. In employing the LoW, this can be accomplished systematically through a work-scanning process.

It is important to note that work support needs to be aligned with work execution. The need for this alignment should be readily apparent. If, for instance, we have a water ballet or medley racing team, we need to provide support in terms of clean and clear water, the best in swim gear, outstanding coaches, etc. Without these environmental influences, the swimmers are not likely to perform well enough to win any competitions for the swim club. Whenever work is not being executed to plan, we need not only to attend to improving work execution (which is what most of us do), but also to improving work support as well.

If work execution and work support are not aligned, then work support required to ensure optimal work execution is haphazard at best, and certainly not what it could be. For instance, a desire to improve work results in the form of a newly formulated performance review intervention—a form of work support—is initiated, but if no real change in work effectiveness occurs, work execution and work support are obviously *not* in alignment.

Other examples frequently found in organizations include new training initiatives that don't significantly improve work execution, reorganizations that result in no improvements, out-of-date software, and so on. On the other hand, reviewing performance—another work support intervention based on operational job models (work execution)—is a perfect example of alignment that can help produce effective work improvement.

In the following illustration, we see once again how work execution can be aligned between work group and jobs using the Work Formula. In essence, the six elements are used to define jobs and work groups in the same way—that is, outputs of the work group to outputs of jobs, inputs to inputs, etc. The six elements of all jobs must be in alignment with the six elements of the work group. Once we have achieved alignment through modeling of work execution between the work group and jobs, we can add alignment to work support that best suit jobs and group work execution. Again, we employ the Work Formula to achieve this alignment. So let's see the typical set of interventions that align work support with work execution.

The Alignment of Work Execution and Work Support

Language of Work™

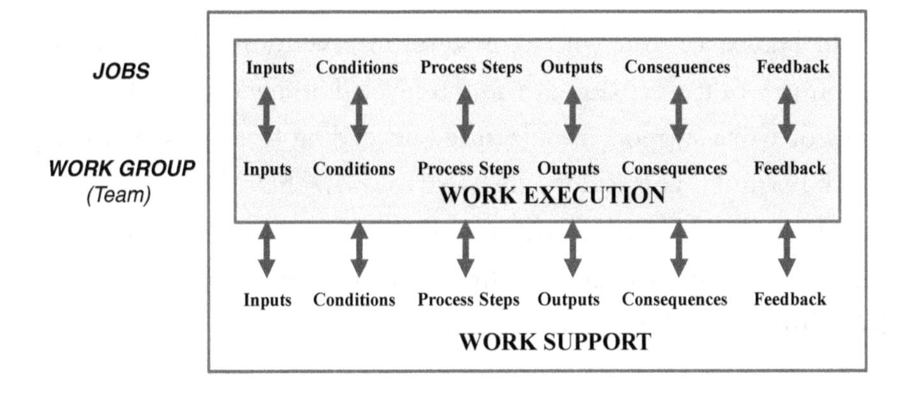

Work Support Matrix

Work support requires a wide range of organizationally established resources—what we call the interventions designed to help get work done in an organization—to assure a healthy work environment. Their presence or absence will say a great deal about the "culture" of an organization. (Culture is loosely defined here as "the way an organization supports doing things around here.") When the support is weak, work usually suffers. When the support is strong, work thrives.

The authors, working with many enterprises, have compiled a fairly complete list of the interventions that usually make up a healthy organization's work support. We will illustrate a few of these work support interventions as they relate to your management role; others you can learn more about in our other published resources. Let's look first at what typically constitutes work support for jobs and work groups, and then at how to access and improve work support in your management role.

In Figure 18 you will see several interventions that assist in enabling work execution at the job level. These various interventions of work support are classified according to the six-element Work Formula. This is done in order to show their direct relationship to and impact on work execution elements of the job. Thus, for instance, you see that for Inputs, work support interventions for job-level work include:

Inputs:

Assignments
Boss/Organization
Equipment/Facilities
Goals & Objectives
Identified Client Needs
Job Description
Strategy

	INPUTS	CONDITIONS	PROCESS STEPS	OUTPUTS	CONSEQUENCES	FEEDBACK
JOB LEVEL	CLIENT NEEDS & RESOURCES	WORK INFLUENCES	WORK METHODS	JOB DELIVERABLES	INDIVIDUAL RESULTS	CONFIRMATIONS & SELF ADJUSTMENT
	Assignments Boss/Organization Equipment/Facilities Goals & Objectives Identified Client Needs Job Description Strategy	Attributes Benefits/Pay Budget Ergonomics Employee Handbook Ethics Policies Safety Schedule Workload	Career Development Plan Documentation Performance Improvement Interventions Skill Maint./Devel. Succession Planning Work Flow Work Tools	Job Models Individual unit: • Knowledge • Products • Services	Customer Satisfaction Job Satisfaction Personal Satisfaction Tie to Work Group	Dialogue Internal Client Evaluations Performance Appraisal Rewards & Recognition Turnover

Figure 18

Note: Your organization may have specific interventions, such as "all hands meetings," which you can add to this list to tailor it to your business.

Thus, to support the work at a job level, one needs (1) clear assignments that provide specific expected outputs and desired consequences, as well as how they should be accomplished and with whom; (2) a level of management that will assist/facilitate work; (3) the right equipment and facilities, and so forth as listed.

The question to ask yourself, as with any of the various interventions of work support is, "How is providing any of these interventions important to the individual in getting their work done effectively and efficiently in our company/organization?" Put another way, "How does ***not*** providing these interventions adversely affect getting a job done?" The way to use this list is to ask, "How does this list help me to understand how to create a culture to support the work of my staff?"

You may want to take the time here to review the interventions your organization provides in support of individual jobs in terms of work inputs, conditions, process steps, outputs, consequences, and feedback. Think of situations you have encountered to see if work support was missing for employees, and how it impacted work execution.

Figure 19 lists the interventions that usually support work execution of work groups, such as your department. Here we find a similar but different list of interventions that support work groups, again listed according to the six elements of work. For example, for Feedback you find the following interventions for work support:

Feedback

Continuous Improvement
Facilitation Methods
Information Systems
Measurements
Meetings

	INPUTS	CONDITIONS	PROCESS STEPS	OUTPUTS	CONSEQUENCES	FEEDBACK
WORK GROUP LEVEL	CLIENT NEEDS & RESOURCES	VALUES & PRACTICES	INTERFACE/ RELATIONSHIPS	WORK GROUP DELIVERABLES	WORK GROUP DELIVERABLES	MANAGEMENT/TEAMz INFORMATION SYSTEM
Interventions	Business Needs Knowledge Orientation Partners Personnel Projects Strategy	Attributes Budget/Funds Conflict Resolution Decision Authority Ethics Mgmt/Leadership Practices & Expectations Other Group Practices Schedule	Management System Partnerships Performance Improvement Interventions Personnel Selection Skill Maint./Devel. Workflow Work Group Ties	Work Group Models Plans: • Knowledge • Products • Services	Client Retention Goal Consistency Across Units Repeat Business Reputation Teamwork	Continuous Improvements Facilitation Methods Information Systems Measurements Meetings

Figure 19

As with the support needed for individual jobs, you need to ask yourself the question, "What effect does ***not*** providing these interventions have on group work efficiency and effectiveness?" For example, not providing a means for the work force to express their work improvement ideas would adversely affect how the current and future work is accomplished. Similarly, if you don't provide reinforcement on work performance, you can expect a drop-off in motivation and overall work output. Review the other interventions/resources that are needed at the work group level for inputs, conditions, process steps, outputs and consequences and ask yourself how these impact work execution.

The numerous interventions of work support captured in Figures 18 and 19 are two of four parts of what we call in the Language of Work the "Work Support Matrix." You can access a complete copy of this Matrix from the authors through their website or you will find one as Figure 23 of *The Business Model* book. There you will find work support needed at the core process and business unit levels.

Chapter 7

The Managing Model: Applying the Work Formula to Facilitate Work

How can the Language of Work be used to manage your department better...and make you stand out? The Managing Model introduces several practical possibilities based on the Work Formula.

It seems that no matter how many courses, books, and workshops we may have experienced, we are rarely prepared for the complexities of a managerial position. While the people-oriented person might find the human side relatively easy, such a person is often buffaloed by the need to be systematic in managing a team. On the other hand, the highly technical managers may well find the people side frustrating. Managing—or as the authors prefer, facilitating—a department is a multifaceted and complex undertaking. People are often thrust into the job with little or no actual management talent or training. Instead it is the technically exemplary job performer who is thought to be the ideal manager. This logic does not necessarily hold, as virtually any new manager soon realizes. (In my own experience, it felt like I was drinking from the proverbial fire hydrant.) The Work Formula can dramatically improve managerial practice for both kinds of managers.

One reason managing is so complex is that in a modern corporation there are so many different functions to perform, each often with its own paperwork and techniques. There is one approach for handling employee issues; another for planning, monitoring, and adjusting the work or project; still another for giving feedback to employees; and another for problem solving. Even that list covers only a few of the roles and responsibilities of a manager. Wouldn't it be great if a significant portion of these could be addressed using a single, flexible approach to work facilitation? That is the goal, if not the direct result, of organizing work execution and support based on the Language of Work. In this chapter we will address a sample of your managing functions, showing how they can be aided through the use of the Work Formula.

Many authors have written about how to manage. Generally these articles and books are about principles to be followed or goals to be realized. Our method is far more operationally focused. Management is not an abstraction; it is a series of day-by-day experiences to achieve primarily results. Therefore, it will come as no surprise that we will introduce managing by presenting first a job model for you as a manager, then for your team as a work group.

The most functional description of your work as a manager would naturally be your specific job model. We can't realize that here specifically in terms of your work situation, but we can present a generic manager's job model. It is built on various manager job models that we have defined in several industries. You can tailor this one to fit yourself, adding any technical deliverables for which you are accountable. Here we will focus solely on the managerial functions.

In Figures 20 through 24, you find a manager's job model using the six-element Work Formula. You will find seven major outputs with associated inputs, conditions, process steps, consequences, and feedback. This job model also has associated skills, knowledge, and attributes that we have chosen *not* to include here since they are not directly germane to what we will be presenting. You can download them for free from our website: www.performancein-ternational.com. Our need here is to emphasize the functions normally included in the job role "Manager."

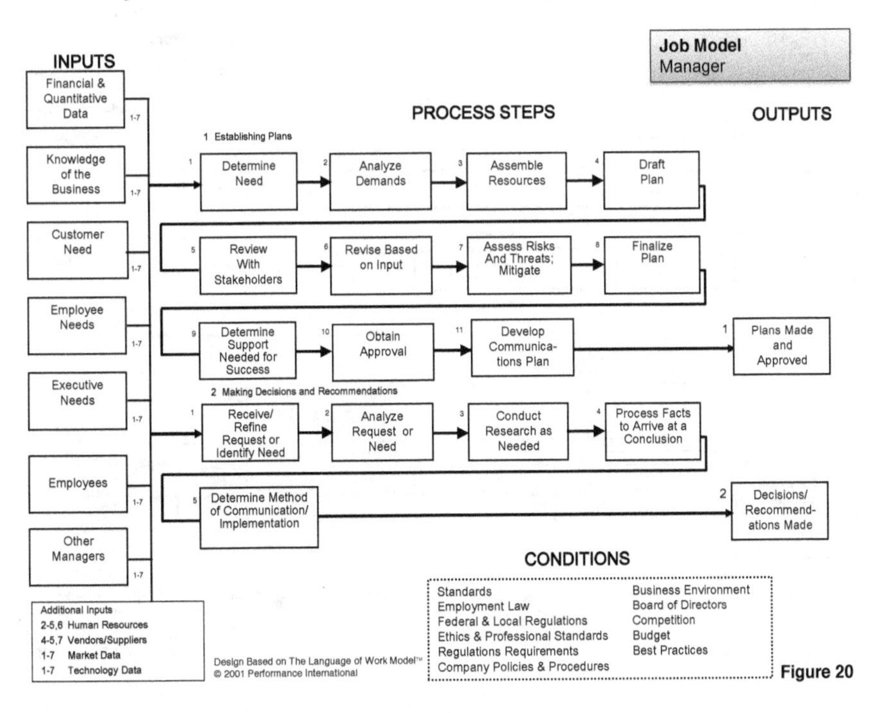

Figure 20

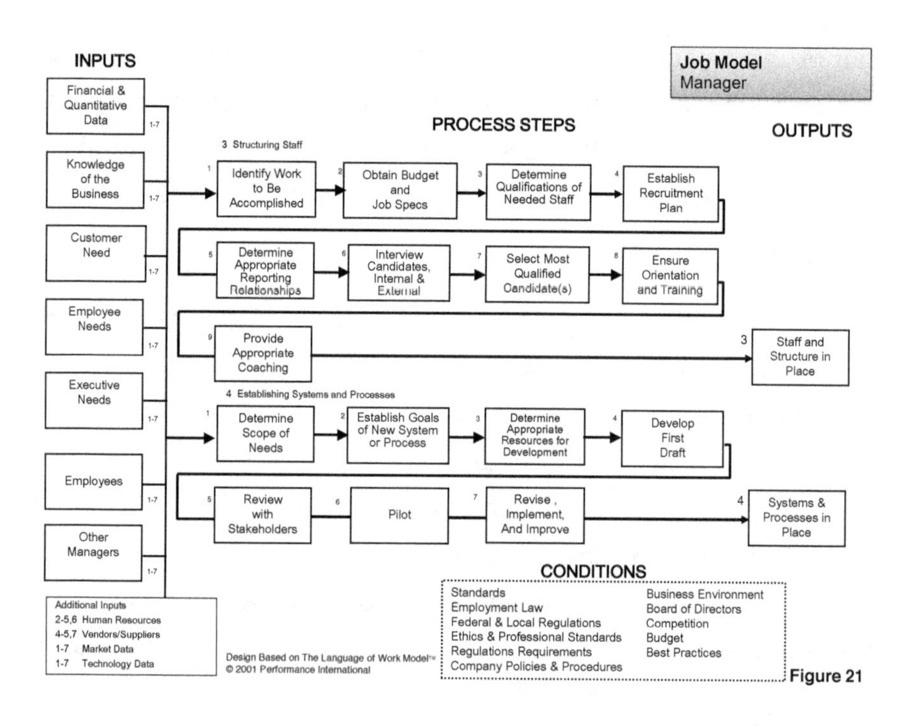

Figure 21

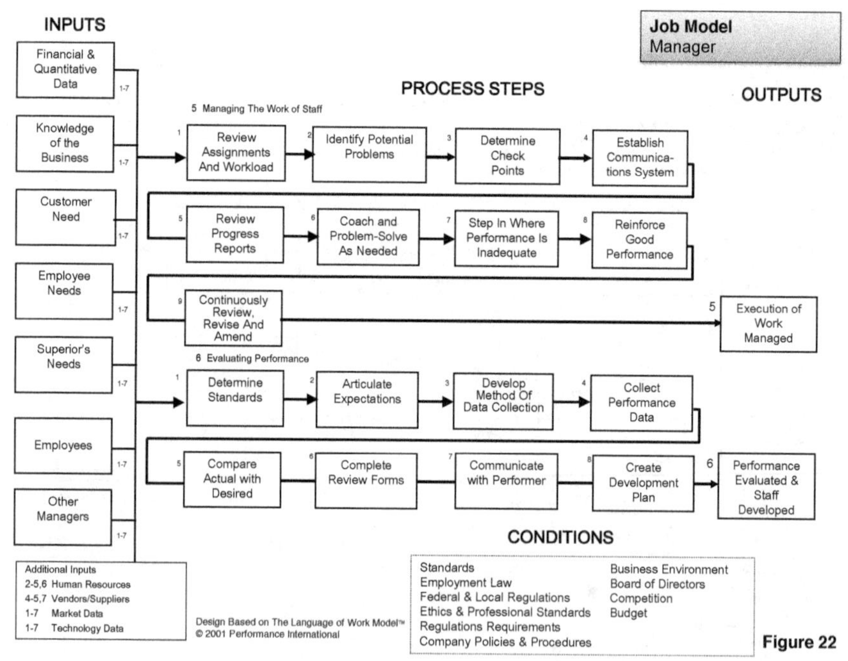

Figure 22

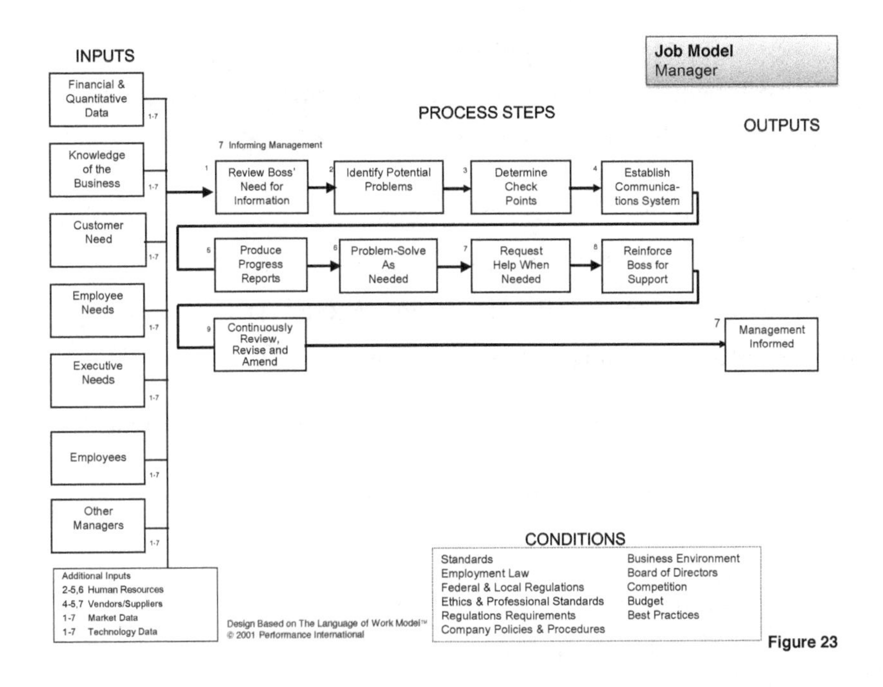

Figure 23

Job Model
Manager

CONSEQUENCES

1. Achieve department goals and objectives commensurate with business mission (outputs 1-7)
2. Customer Satisfaction (outputs 1-7)
3. Management approval (outputs 1-7)
4. Budgetary compliance and efficiency (outputs 1-5, 7)
5. Staff efficiency and development (output 6)
6. Employee satisfaction (outputs 1-3,5,7)
7. Safe work environment maintained (outputs 4, 5)

FEEDBACK

During

1. Client
2. Management
3. Peers
4. Staff
5. Clients/Customers
6. Suppliers & Vendors
7. Results
8. External Experts

After

1. Client
2. Management
3. Peers
4. Staff
5. Clients/Customers
6. Results

Design Based on The Language of Work Model™

Figure 24

You will probably find most of the management functions that you are currently performing shown in this job model. You can add others to clarify your job situation, expectations, and activities.

Because so much of the manager's job relates to the employees being managed, we have summarized and organized those functions into what we refer to as the "Managing Model" (Figure 25), or what we also refer to generically as the Manager/Worker Interface.

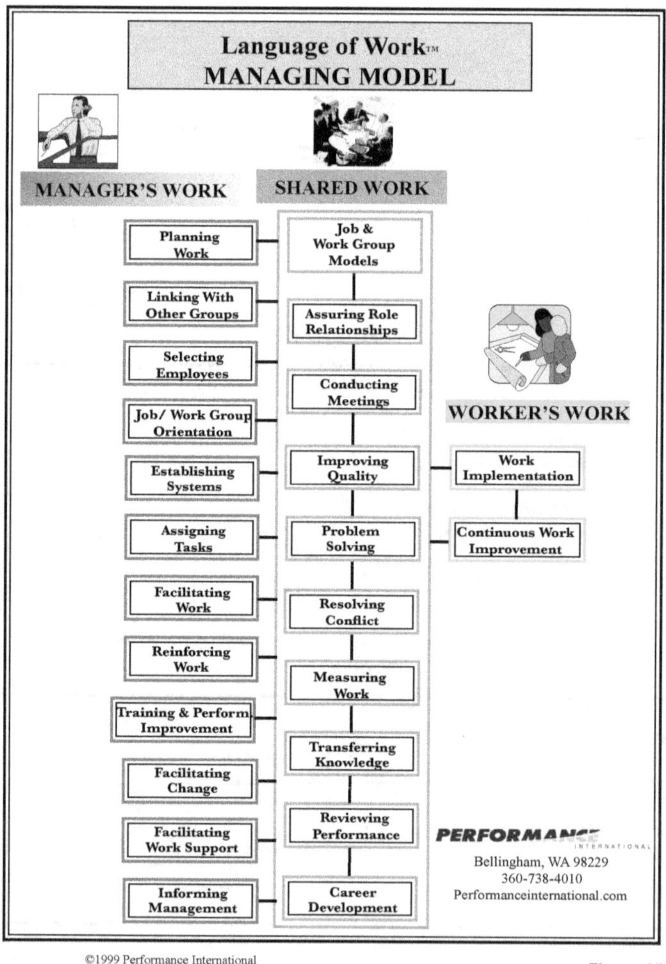

©1999 Performance International

Figure 25

Figure 25 divides the manager's job into three categories:

1. those functions you *solely* or (nearly solely) do yourself,
2. those you do *with* the workforce, and
3. those that the workforce primarily performs, but for which you are ultimately responsible.

Within each category there are several roles or work functions. The manager performs those roles listed in the left column pretty much alone. These include planning, selecting employees, establishing systems, and the like. The second category, what managers often do with the workforce, are listed in the middle column. Thus, *together* you define job models, hold meetings, solve problems, and the like. And, finally, the workers have functions they perform pretty much on their own, and these are listed in the right column. This isn't to say that the line between what you do alone, with others, and as a leader is always that clearly demarcated, nor should it be. Most work is essentially collaborative. We encourage you to find, in addition to the functions listed here, how the Work Formula may be used to enhance facilitation in other ways.

So far, as a manager, you have hopefully come to a fuller understanding of work and how to define or model it (Chapters 2 through 5), and how to fully support that work (Chapter 6) by establishing and assuring a healthy work environment. In this chapter you are learning how to manage that work using the same Work Formula.

Since the LoW represents a behavioral approach to work, it follows that using the Work Formula can make your own work, and the behavior (another word for work) of employees, more effective.

We will illustrate how to use the Work Formula to implement the various managerial functions listed in Figure 25. In doing so, this should also provide insight into using the Work Formula to implement other management functions you may be responsible for. In our work we are constantly finding other uses for the Language of Work, and we know you will as well. We hope you will one day share these applications with us.

MANAGER'S WORK

The functions in "Manager's Work" as identified in *The Managing Model*, represent, in general terms, the facilitation that a manager is primarily responsible for on his/her own. Later we will consider those he or she performs in a shared relationship with the work group/team. Of course, virtually any managerial function is best done in concert with workers if for no other reason than to solicit their buy-in to whatever is needed for efficient and effective work implementation. Therefore, while the following are identified as the "Manager's Work," they all have elements of inclusion of anyone and all who would help the manager achieve the work.

Planning Work

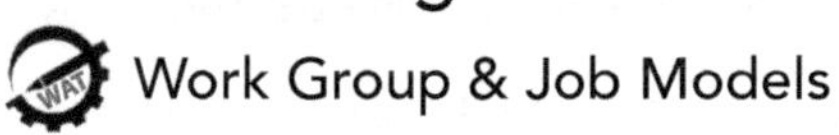

Have you ever…

- found it difficult to plan the work of your department or for individuals within it?
- found it hard to plan work of individuals in light of one another?
- been uncertain when and where to set milestones?

It's a bit simplistic, but true, to say that effectively and efficiently planning of work is mostly knowing clearly what the work is in the first place. If the LoW achieves anything, it is clarity among all parties doing the work as to what the work is using the same terms to do so. The Work Group Model that defines your department or team work is quite clear on what is to be produced (outputs and consequences) and how it will do so (inputs, conditions, process steps, and feedback). The same is true and consistent with individual work using various job models. A model can even delineate clearly how that work will be supported, what standards are expected, what human relations factors are important, and what the financial support will be. Given this, then planning how much of that work, through what time period, communicated with whom, and so on should be pretty straightforward. If it's team work, then use the Work Group Model. If it's individual work, use the Job Model.

Linking with Others

Linking with Others, in this context, has to do with your group's relationship with other work groups (as contrasted solely with role relationships within your work group that is also part of the Manager/Worker Interface diagram, which we will describe later).

As a manager, you are often responsible for a honeycomb of interrelated work between your department and other groups. Members of the marketing group interact with production and sales. The training group interacts with content experts. Distribution interacts with production. IT, HR, accounting, and other staff groups interact with all line departments.

When the inputs your department receives—others' outputs—from another department are late, for example, your department's work is negatively affected. Then, when your department's output does not meet standards, the next department's work is affected in terms of timeliness, quality, cost, and/or perhaps quantity. Such linkages between work groups need to be clear to prevent one unit from holding another up or adversely affecting the others' work. Showing the linkages clearly so that everyone understands the cause-and-effect relationship they have with each other is critical to the success of not only your department, but the total enterprise.

Using the various forms (work execution levels) of Language of Work models as the basis for linking work with others, we have found, consistently changes the tone and tenor of work-sharing discussions. This is primarily because when models of core processes or work groups are shared between managers and workers, any discussion can be centered objectively on specific elements of the work rather than on the generalities of work relationships and issues. This is critical to reaching solutions that improve effectiveness and efficiency of work, let alone relationships. While other resources (especially Langdon, 2014) on defining core processes as a precursor to identifying jobs is one way this can be done, here we will concern ourselves with making clear the relationships you have with other groups primarily through shared work group models.

When your work group and other groups have been modeled using the LoW, you are in a position to see and discuss the linkages between them in ways never before possible. There are several dimensions upon which to hold these discussions and make sure things are going as hoped and planned. These include, but are not limited to the work relationships between groups in terms of:

- Shared consequences
- The interdepartmental input/output relationship
- Shared process steps
- Mutual feedback
- Shared work conditions

A brief description of these will help you to better link your department with others.

When you compare your work group model with other work groups, you'll first note that you often share common consequences to achieve even though you are producing fundamentally different outputs. This might be as generic as a shared "customer satisfaction," or a more specific consequence related to the quality of a product or service. Then you will see how your group outputs become others' inputs and their outputs become your inputs. Or you'll clearly discern that you share steps from a core process or within process steps of your separate work group models. And finally, you'll see that some of your feedback emanates from other work groups, individuals, or shared sources of information such as audits, measurements, and the like. Having total clarity about such linkages is important to you, those you interact with, and the company as a whole.

As an example of linking relationships in a market research firm we worked with, researchers worked in movie theaters on Wednesdays and Thursdays. They approached moviegoers about their reaction to various ads. They asked questions like, "Would you see this movie based on this ad?" This raw data was turned over to data analyzers, who compared answers by demographic group—age, gender, socioeconomic status, sources of information, etc. The analyzers then had to write reports that could be given to the client, who would make decisions about the marketing strategy for each movie based on the data analysis.

So the first group's output was "Data collected." This served as input to the data analyzers. Their output was "Analyzed data," which in turn served as input to the client, whose output was "Decisions made." Those decisions, in turn, served as input to the media staff who placed ads in various media.

The main consequence everyone was trying to achieve was "highest box office receipts for opening weekend." When viewed this way, it is easy to see the relationship of each group's work to the others. Before coming to this insight, each team had blamed the other for being "so slow," "What a group of morons," "Can't anybody get it right anymore?" Once the teams had worked through their work group and process models, and saw their relationship in black and white, tensions were reduced. The whole group looked at ways they could support each other in accomplishing the work on time and to the standard of quality needed. The cost of the process was reduced by 10%, and the effectiveness was improved by 20%.

You can see that the Language of Work allows everyone to link work needs better at the work group level; then making improvements systematically using the same model of work is much easier. This is because, in our experience, this approach removes much of the emotion that can plague such discussions on work linkage. Stubborn refusal to move forward is avoided because the data about the work is in black and white in front of everyone involved. Work clarity is achieved at levels never before realized. Even individual personalities and ways of doing work play a much smaller part when work group models are the focus of the discussion. The resolution of conflicts is centered on meeting common client needs and consequences, eliminating "I'm right/you're wrong" or "I'm up/you're down" thinking that permeates most work discussions.

As a final thought on work linkage, a long-time friend and colleague of ours coined a very useful phrase when it comes to managing work linkages both within and between work groups. In "Managing the White Space," Dr. Geary Rummler (1990) noted that facilitating work done by those we manage is as much about what happens between the elements of work as it is with each individual and collective act of work. Thus as managers we must be concerned with, for example, not just what each person or group does itself, but how that work is handed off to others who in turn depend on its quality. As managers we must carefully know, observe, and attend to those points of handoff to assure that they are done well. Where this is not so, we must know how to facilitate or manage them so they become efficient and effective. Knowing exactly where and what the linkages are and attending to them will help you manage the white spaces.

Selecting Employees

Have you ever…

- found it difficult to select the right person for the job?
- found it hard to tell HR exactly what kind of worker to look for?
- based hiring solely on that gut feeling that this person is the right one?
- relied mostly on someone else's recommendation for hiring?
- needed to know what it would take to get a candidate up to speed?

Finding the right person for a job can be difficult. Typically, selections are made with some vague idea of the work found in a job description (which often includes a wish list of unmeasurable attributes), some idea of the skills and knowledge the individual should bring to the work, and a gut feeling about the personality and makeup of the candidate being interviewed. Everyone then waits to see what happens. Sometimes we are right, and sometimes we are wrong. Given that it is quite an investment in the screening, interviewing, and initial tryout of new employees, anything that would improve the process of employee selection will save time, money, frustration, and certainly improve job or team performance. Using the information from job models turns out to be an answer long overdue.

To begin with, job models reflect what is to be produced and how. Instead of asking vague questions about their experience, would-be employees can be asked what experience they have in producing specific outputs and achieving the consequences reflected in the job model. Asking how they produced these outputs can help you find what experience they have in doing the process steps you want done. You can also ask which inputs, conditions, and feedback they found useful. Then you can ask about the skills and knowledge they bring to the job. All these factors are specified in the job model and can be prompts as to what to ask both the applicant and perhaps his or her references.

In conducting the actual face-to-face interview, always ask the applicant to describe what they did; not what they *would* do. The specificity of the job model allows you to assess specific knowledge and experience of the individual. Here, the past is key to the future.

One of the other seemingly minor parts of a job model that we gave reference to only briefly before, comes to play here as a major component of employee selection. You will recall that modeling is done with exemplary performers of these jobs, and that it would be wise to identify the so-called "attributes" of the job. This can be done in general terms by asking exemplary performers to identify desirable attributes, or by more systematically using some form of survey such as the Kolbe (2003) Index. The list of attributes needed as innate qualities for each job will make it likely you and HR can better select candidates. Some have suggested, by the way, that the attribute indicators are perhaps more reliable than more conventional means in selecting for eventual success.

Job/Work Group Orientation

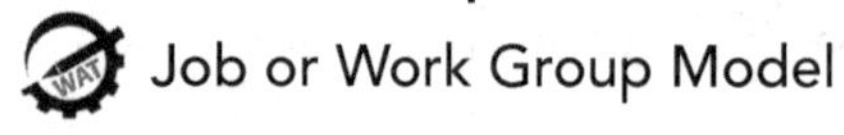

Orientation is that important aspect of acquainting new employees, experienced or not, with their specific job duties. Using an individual Job Model for this purpose should go without saying.

What job models have that a job description lacks is the "how" of the work role. Most orientations, if really done at all, are a presentation of job expectations—only outcomes if you will. Or they get into the details of work execution without orientation to the bigger picture of a job. True, the job is really mostly about, "How should the person do his or her job?" For this you need a clear explanation of what consequences they are supposed to achieve and what outputs will realize these consequences. Then indicate what inputs trigger the work, what resources will be utilized, what rules and regulations must be adhered to, what procedures should be followed, and what communication during and after will aid in doing work right and on time. These are all part of using a Job Model as the WAT to aid orientation. It's a convenient and targeted point of reference for knowing what to say during an orientation (or any other role clarification, assignment, etc.). Also, one can note where the challenges and pitfalls are in a job, where to devote one's attention, resource issues, and so on.

As an added suggestion to orientation using a Job Model, an introduction to the skills and knowledge—both strengths and needed improvement—is recommended. Thus, the manager should review the skills and knowledge specified in the Job Model with a worker so that they have a clear path for what they should do to further assure success.

Another question is, "What things can the worker do to improve the chances of success immediately and into the future?" In addition to this, in a subsequent chapter, we shall note the importance of using a Work Group Model as part of role orientation both inside and outside your team.

Establishing Systems

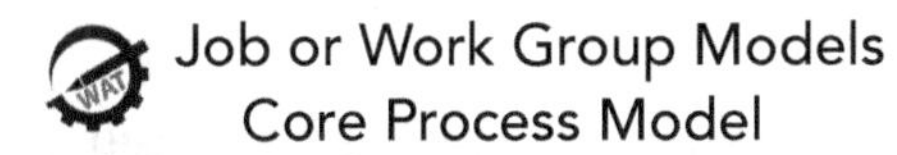

Have you ever...

- found it difficult to translate a new company process into specifications for workers to be able to use in their job?
- felt that the company was taking too much time and money to make changes in work processes?
- wanted to establish a standard way of doing some aspect of work, but didn't know how to go about it?

Systems are the standard procedures and processes that the work force is to follow in executing work. Most of these "systems" are already implicit in the job and work group models that you will have for your department if you follow the LoW. There are systems established/required by others, such as HR, IT, quality control, etc. If any of these (or new) systems are desired and under your control—such as the installation of new software or hardware—you might consider using the LoW to identify, establish, or improve these systems. We have, for example, aided many enterprises in the operationalizing of enterprise-wide software systems, such as Oracle and SAP. This has generally taken the form of modeling their core processes and jobs to make clear the changes needed in the revised or new job. Models are both tools for doing work analysis and highly useful in implementing and operationalizing needed changes.

Assigning Tasks

Job or Work Group Models

Have you ever...

- felt that some workers just never "get" what you ask them to do?
- felt that you have to repeat what to do over and over?
- wished people would ask more questions when things are not going right, so you could help before the problem grew?

Using models that are part of the Language of Work when assigning tasks to individuals and groups greatly enhances your effectiveness.

Because the LoW employs all the elements that constitute work execution, you can provide clarity by beginning with the output expected. Reviewing the consequences, inputs, conditions, process steps, and feedback can then engage the employees in a meaningful and shared exchange leading to total work understanding. Good questions, focused on a particular "box" or element in the model, can be answered easily. If obstacles to understanding are identified by the employee, you as manager can facilitate a good problem-solving discussion immediately.

We recently saw this happen in a case where one employee had problems doing invoicing because of the deadline required. Another employee would have to do double work to complete the task. They negotiated back and forth, each identifying specific issues, until they found a solution. It was wonderful to see the clarity that resulted. This approach allows you, as the manager of the group, to facilitate success instead of being a dictatorial figure making demands. This approach also lets employees to work together to achieve clarity, commitment, and understanding.

Because the LoW also includes Work Support, it is possible for you and the team to identify additional needs (such as job aids or different compensation schemes) when needed. If clarity exists and tasks are still not completed timely or well, then an audit of the Work Support matrix may identify additional actions you need to take.

Facilitating Work

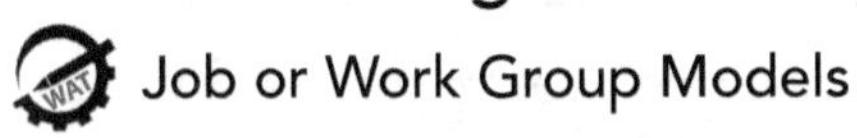

Have you ever…

- failed to help individuals or teams before big problems arose?
- thought you could have been more proactive in assisting team effort?
- failed to talk to others outside your group about the ways they could help your team be more effective or efficient?

Think of any of the work models or matrices (at any level or layer in the LoW) as a kind of dashboard that you can monitor and use to affect what is going on. You can do this continuously. For instance, you can monitor the processes, the timing, and the quality of inputs that are being delivered to your work group. This is an essential managerial function that has been difficult or impossible to consistently monitor in the past. Your job requires providing resources to do the work; now you can more adequately support your team in this regard.

Similarly, you could also observe whether people are following the conditions of the work. If not, you can facilitate and reinforce compliance through appropriate feedback. You can hold a problem-solving discussion regarding conditions. One manager we worked with, for example, found that employees had no access to the rules they needed to follow. Making the rules available solved a number of problems.

Each of the other elements of work execution and support must be monitored. Then, when issues are identified, you can determine if the employees can solve the issues themselves, or if you need to facilitate the situation. Sometimes they forget to perform steps in the process; other times they need new skills. At still other times you need to help them by reinforcing (one kind of feedback) their new performance.

Employees, by themselves, cannot always assure that others will deliver the appropriate quantity or quality outputs to them in a timely way because they are not in control of all aspects of their work. Then they may be deprived of the inputs necessary to do the work. You may have to facilitate a solution to this for them. Having the work models to constantly show you what's going on is your guide to facilitation.

Reinforcing Work Performance

Have you ever…

- failed to give credit where credit was due?
- failed to recognize others for their contributions?
- failed to achieve the kind of efficiency you desire for your team?
- only given credit after the work is finished, rather than during the time it is being accomplished?

As a manager, you need to provide regular feedback to your team (and annual performance reviews do not totally suffice). Yet providing timely and effective feedback to employees on their work is sorely lacking in American business. Since the work group and job models clearly define the sources of needed feedback, you can monitor the various kinds of feedback for use in your unit. You should, as well, encourage employees to monitor and use the various kinds of feedback explicit in their own job models.

There are two things to keep in mind:

First, people need feedback as they do the work. This encourages ongoing effective performance. Correction along the way is more efficient than re-work when a deliverable is unsatisfactory. Waiting until the work is finished may mean a lost opportunity, as well as an upset internal or external client. This could lead to blaming you, the manager, because you are, after all, the chief encourager/motivator of your group's work.

Second, the feedback that occurs after the work is complete is the ultimate test of everyone's work, including yours as a manager. Delivering outputs to achieve consequences is what work (and competence) is all about. Thus, the client/customer gives feedback, both positive and negative. But if it is negative, how well and how fast you and others respond will speak volumes to your external customers. This response will govern their ultimate satisfaction and affect repeat business. Unhappy customers can be retained provided you listen, care, and act.

A manager needs to have a method in place to continuously reach out to measure satisfaction, see that employees learn from it, are reinforced for doing so, and are responsive to customers. Your success and that of your workers depends on successful utilization of feedback to improve overall individual and team performance.

Training & Performance Improvement

Job Model

Have you ever…

- wondered if the training you suggested for someone will really meet the need?
- wondered why HR has a course or program that makes no sense to you?
- just had difficulty deciding what training to suggest?
- if there are ways to improve performance besides training?

Training and performance improvement for jobs, work group, and core processes are necessary. But, these efforts are time consuming and possibly take away from work execution. Thus the question becomes, "What training (and what performance improvement programs) really meet management's and workers' needs?" or "What works?" or "How can I describe my need so clearly that others design real solutions to meet my (and my team's) needs?"

Experience shows that training, while often producing positive results, has not always been efficient or cost effective. Nor does it respond to work changes rapidly enough. Where is the problem? Is it with Training Departments that offer the programs they think are necessary? Is the answer a different medium? Or is the problem with management's inability to specify what training they really need? Or might it be a combination of these?

There are two sources for knowing what training and other performance improvement efforts would be effective. And both sources should originate from management, because managers can look across the work force to see the common performance improvement needs. To date, tools that quickly communicated needs were missing. Management should have methods to identify such needs that are practical, accurate, and quick. And, rather than relying on a training department to figure this out for you, you should be doing it—it's your job.

One of the two sources has already been described—the performance review. When conducted periodically—at least twice a year—to assess ongoing and future work needs (such as prescribed in job models) work improvement information is being continually provided to HR and other internal change agents. They should be able to review that data to decide what training and other performance improvement interventions might be required.

The second suggestion is an online assessment across the work force, such as a survey supported by management and administered by HR to identify performance improvement needs. Not all the work force need be involved in such online assessments, but at least a representative sample such that accurate results can be projected. In this kind of assessment, the job models serve as the source of data to be evaluated. There can be three levels of data to be measured: work execution, skills/knowledge, and/or competencies. The work execution evaluation uses an assessment of process steps, inputs, conditions and feedback. The skills/knowledge assessment asks employees and/or managers to rate levels of specific skills or knowledge needed to perform work. The competencies typically use a 360^0 or 180^0 evaluation.

The purpose of across-the-work-force assessments such as suggested here is to identify cross-functional, as well as work-group-specific performance improvement needs designed to achieve economies of scale across the organization. While performance reviews identify individual needs for work improvement (and can lead to robust personal development programs), the broader assessments of the work force lead to identification of needs throughout the organization.

Facilitating Change

Job or Work Group Model

Have you ever…

- not known how to actualize a needed change in technology, process, the culture, or other such effort at the job or team level?

- felt that you didn't know how to support an organizational change?
- had difficulty getting a change to stick?
- had difficulty explaining a change to individual workers or the team?
- felt that making a desired change in technology or culture took far too much time, effort, or money?

Work constantly changes, and it seems to do so more as competition increases, markets change, and technology evolves. To date, there has not been a reliable way to respond quickly to these changes—especially at the job level—although many an organization has tried by spending lots of money and time. Some organizations have gone so far as to eliminate the standard job descriptions because situations changed too rapidly for them to stay current. This is less than ideal because it does not provide a critical aspect of work support that employees need. It is, rather, short-term thinking that hampers long-term success. Using job descriptions as agents of change made sense before job models were first developed some 20 years ago, but job descriptions were often vague and unwieldy. Job and work group models, however, can be significant in making effective change happen quickly and seamlessly.

We have already established that job or work group models are highly functional for communicating what the work is, then evaluating and improving it. They can also be used to clarify and operationalize changes. When work or culture changes, the changes can be indicated on the job model. This helps concretize the changes and shows the difference between the current way of doing a job and the desired way.

Where job holders know and use their "present" or their AS IS job model, then a new, revised TO BE model can be developed showing the effects of the changes. This creates a context for change that aids overall communication regarding how the work changes and the effects it will have. It also serves as a guidepost for observation and measurement—checking whether changes have indeed occurred or if legacy systems are still in place. The functionality of work change made possible by the job model is crucial for the manager responsible.

Needed changes in work often, but not exclusively, also manifest themselves by the revision to an existing, or introduction of a new, core process across many work groups. These come about, for instance, in response to the introduction of enterprise-wide software. Tools executives use for analyzing change are often not useful for those who have to perform the changes, let alone for those, such as trainers, who aid them. Following executive process mapping, the manager's concern inevitably becomes how to actualize such process changes at the team or job level. A review of the process map as the training component, in our experience, hasn't effectively worked. So what's the alternative?

Let us look again at the example of a previous job model sample, the Business Analyst, from Chapter 4. Here, in Figures 26 and 27 (identical to Figures 14 and 15) are two representative pages of a job model that we now call the AS IS Business Analyst job model.

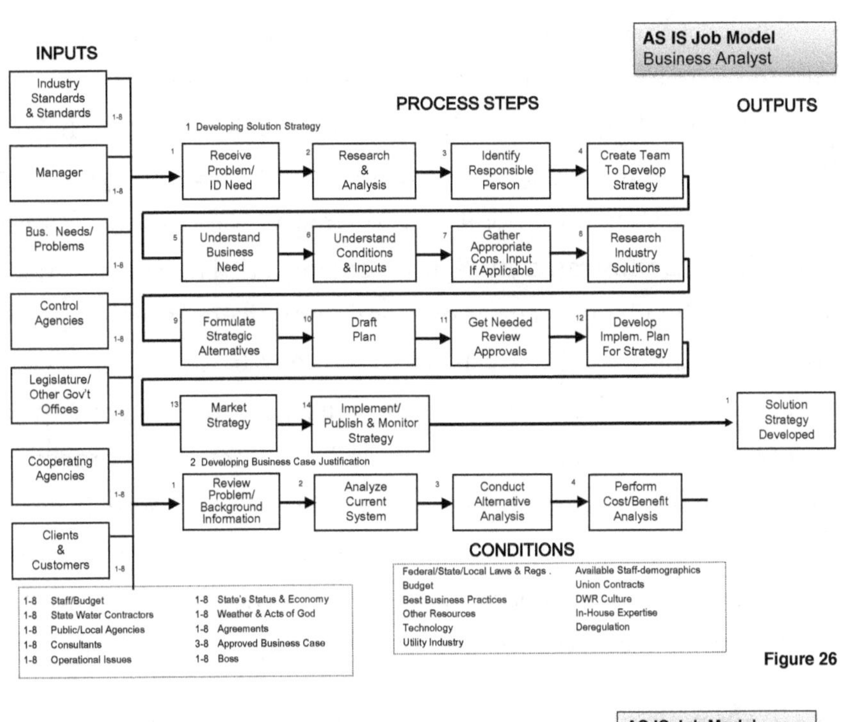

Figure 26

AS IS Job Model
Business Analyst

CONSEQUENCES

1. Contributing to viability of Water Resources Agency (outputs 1-8)
2. Integrated system (outputs 1-8)
3. Satisfied customers (outputs 1-8)
4. Cost effectiveness (outputs 1-8)
5. Increased effectiveness and efficiency of IT (outputs 1-8)
6. Changed paradigm (outputs 1-8)
7. Problems solved (outputs 1-8)
8. Informed/skilled users (outputs 3-4)
9. Process improvements (outputs 1-8)
10. Automation of processes (outputs 1-8)
11. Supporting compliance of laws (outputs 1-8)
12. Increased decision support (outputs 1-8)

FEEDBACK

During

1. External Customers
2. System Tools
3. Control Agencies
4. User/Clients
5. Process Owners
6. Executive Management
7. System Performance
8. Vendors
9. Consultants
10. Other Integrated Functional Areas
11. Peers

After

1. Public/Media
2. System Tools
3. Control Agencies
4. User/Clients
5. Process Owners
6. Executive Management
7. System Performance
8. Vendors
9. Consultants
10. Peers
11. External Customers

Figure 27

The AS IS job model reflects the current job before the introduction of a change. For example, we'll use in this case the introduction of Agile methodology. You might say that the AS IS represents the "legacy" system for the business analysts. The changes have been incorporated into what we label as the TO BE job model, as illustrated in Figures 28 and 29. The source documents for the changes come predominately from "swim-lane" or other such analyses. If one has used the LoW to define these core processes, there is the advantage, of course, of closer alignment to changes in job or work group models. When base core processes are LoW-modeled, the jobs or work groups that will actualize the needed changes are defined and aligned to the core process(es) using the same Work Formula. Let's see some change examples for the business analyst position that is going Agile.

To show the changes, based on the core process mapping, you can ask a series of questions about the changes and reflect these in the new TO BE job model. A Work Analytics Tool (see Figures 36 and 37) to be introduced in Chapter 9 will introduce questions to be asked, such as:

1. Will any of the outputs of the job be eliminated or changed?
2. Are there new or changing consequences? How would these be stated, and which outputs produce the changed consequences?
3. What process steps are impacted and how?
4. What inputs are impacted and how?
5. What conditions change?
6. What feedback changes, and how?

7. Is there any work support that needs to be established or changed to help do the changes more effectively and efficiently?

Not all answers to these questions will result in changes for a given work element, but many will.

Now let us look at a few examples of business analyst changes when employing Agile, and see how to reflect these in the Job Model.

With the TO BE Job Model in hand, you and others, such as trainers, will be able to identify the precise steps affected by this change. This allows for an excellent discussion, good questions, and a commitment to follow the new process. The discussion also creates an opportunity for the manager to ask, "How would you like to assure me that you are following this new process?" Thus, an added approval step after the research and analysis step might be mutually agreed upon. (Perhaps a simple cc of the report to the manager will suffice.) Besides the primary communication of needed changes for the worker(s), this is just one of the ways the manager's job can be made easier and supportive of change through the presence of AS and TO BE Job Models.

TO BE Job Model Sample

(see next page)

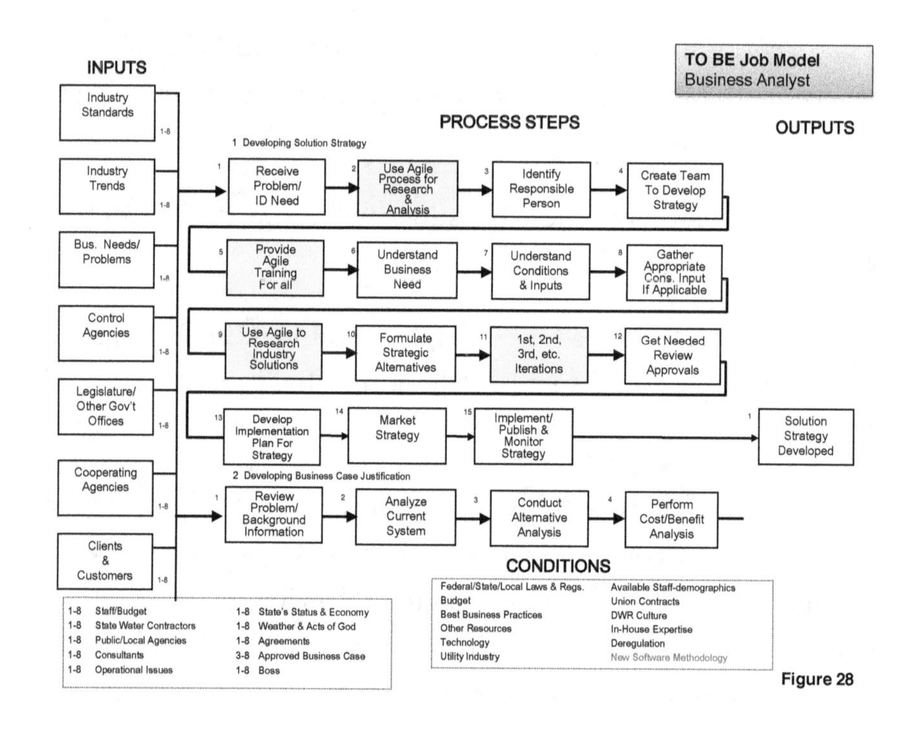

Figure 28

TO BE Job Model
Business Analyst

CONSEQUENCES

1. Contributing to viability of Water Resources Agency (outputs 1-8)
2. Integrated system (outputs 1-8)
3. Satisfied customers (outputs 1-8)
4. Cost effectiveness (outputs 1-8)
5. Increased effectiveness and efficiency of IT (outputs 1-8)
6. Changed paradigm (outputs 1-8)
7. Problems solved (outputs 1-8)
8. Informed/skilled users (outputs 3-4)
9. Process improvements (outputs 1-8)
10. Automation of processes (outputs 1-8)
11. Supporting compliance of laws (outputs 1-8)
12. Increased decision support (outputs 1-8)
13. Faster development time (outputs 1-8)
14. Faster research time (output 6)
15. Ability to enhance testing process (output 3)

FEEDBACK

During

1. External Customers
2. System Tools
3. Control Agencies
4. User/Clients
5. Process Owners
6. Executive Management
7. System Performance
8. Vendors
9. Consultants
10. Other Integrated Functional Areas
11. Peers
12. Scrum Action Item

After

1. Public/Media
2. System Tools
3. Control Agencies
4. User/Clients
5. Process Owners
6. Executive Management
7. System Performance
8. Vendors
9. Consultants
10. Peers
11. External Customers

Figure 29

Here are some additional examples of changes in various work elements from the AS IS state to the TO BE state:

Process Steps Example:
The Research & Analysis, step 2 in developing Solution Strategy in the previously shown Figure 26, will change to utilize a process employing an Agile development. This will require Agile training for all business analysts, and a different approach to researching industry solutions. Also, the way the Draft Plan, step 10 (see Figure 26 again) is developed, reviewed, and revised will be less exacting, while still needing to be in constant dynamic development until it achieves what is desired. These and other aspects of job change from Figure 26 and 27 are color-coded in Figures 28 and 29. Each would be compared for details of the changes to the original core process and related supporting documentation.

Conditions Example:
New software technology will be employed and must be followed. This is color-coded in red.

Consequences Example:
Several new consequences will be realized. These are cross-referenced to the outputs that produce each consequence and are color-coded in red.

Feedback Example:
A new feedback loop will help assure improved team effort in business analysis. This is color-coded in red.

Work Support Example:
An analysis of the Job Model (and core process) would reveal the need for certain types of interventions, including:

- Training
- Team-building
- Documentation Support
- Etc.

You can see that the TO BE Job Model is there to capture needed changes for the worker in a context they understand: moving from the present way of doing things to the new ways. When changes in strategy, technology, culture, or organization are reviewed through the prism of the Job Model (or Work Group Model for teams), employee adoption of the changes is faster and more fully understood. Experience has shown us that resistance is lessened because the change is made concrete and operational. Changes (and training) primarily tied to swim lanes and such often seem overwhelming. We have even seen instances where the AS IS and TO BE approach eliminated a job, and that was totally understood. Employees who saw that the outputs they had been delivering had been eliminated, outsourced, or transferred had relatively little difficulty in moving toward new employment, inside or outside the organization. Instead of resisting an abstract change, they could view the change dispassionately.

Facilitating change is not an intangible notion or a pep rally discussion, nor is it unimportant. But it does require a tangible tool that communicates why a change is needed. A job model serves as that very concrete tool. As their manager, you are now in a much better position to constantly review and assist in such changes from AS IS to TO BE.

SHARED WORK

Assuring Role Relations

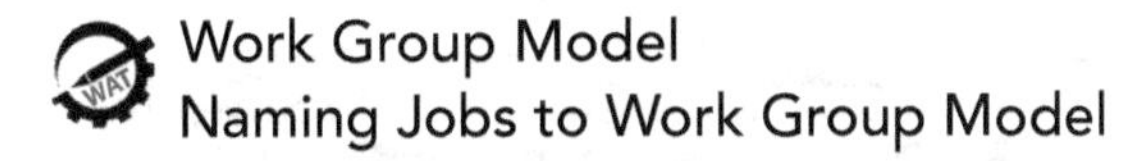

A work group is a team, in large part, because each individual knows both what his or her job is explicitly and how that job relates to others. In the past, all this was intuitive, unseen, and often buried. There has been no way to make these relationships explicit until the advent of job and work group models using the same definition of work—a Work Formula. When relationships could not be made clear to everyone, gossip and personality-based innuendo often resulted. Traditionally, the closest to showing interrelationships among jobs in a work group has been the use of flow or swim-lane diagrams. But even this falls short because it typically only specifies about a third of what work is. Often there is so much detail that individual work gets confused within the core process, while showing no job relationship within a work group. While the work group and job models will provide much clarity to role relationships—for example whose output is someone else's input—we have another WAT that you will find particularly powerful in assuring and quantifying role relationships. It's called Identifying Jobs to Work Group Model.

Once the work group has been modeled, you can name the jobs within the work group, assign a number and/or color to each, and identify what jobs have a role in completing each of the process steps leading to work group outputs. This is illustrated in Figure 30.

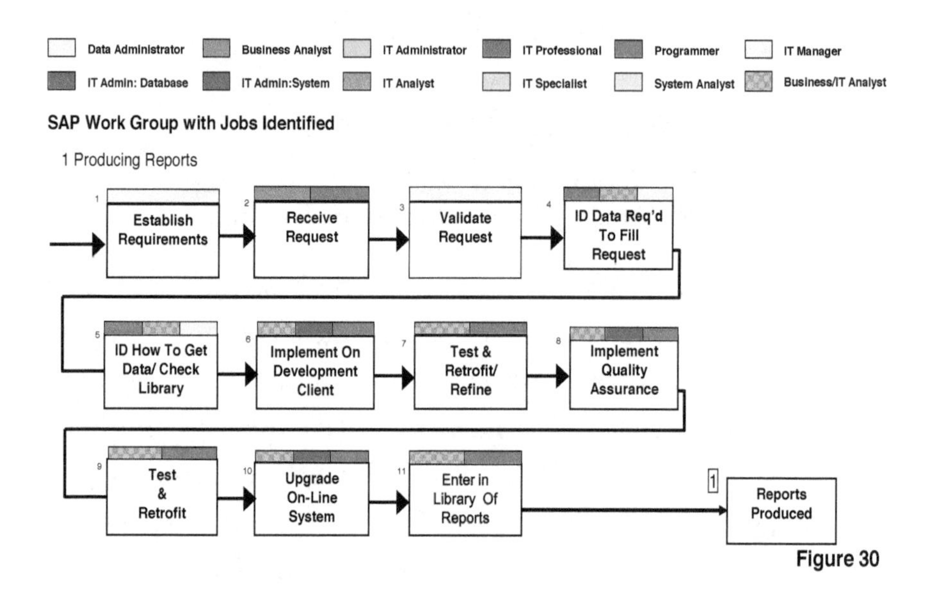

Figure 30

As you see, this model clearly shows who on the team is involved in each step of a given process. (By the way, this model does not, by itself, constitute a job description or task list. Instead, it shows where all the individual jobs are involved in the process. When several people are involved in the same tasks, it is easy to see.) Thus, in step 4 of the process of Producing Report, the programmer, the business analyst, and the data administrator all have a role in "Identifying Data Required to Fill Request." If you are, for example, the programmer, it is quite clear that you have a role in this step and that you share the step with others. You can readily see that you are involved in eight of the eleven steps that produce this output, and you can note all the places you work with others.

The 80/20 rule, and our direct observation of work in hundreds of workplaces, reveals that 80% of the problems occur in 20% of the work. Using a core process or work group model for role relationships helps to pinpoint precisely where any given problem occurs. Instead of arguing, the team can "vote" to identify the problem. Once identified, it is quite easy to then find the problem, revise the process, or develop procedures to clarify the situation.

Each member of the team can identify his or her sole and joint accountabilities within the team. Stress and drama decline considerably when these models are used by teams attempting to successfully deliver outputs to others.

One place where this was used to great value occurred when two different groups had the same job title: Organization Development Specialist (ODS). This position existed in two different departments—one that served the entire corporation and the other that was limited to one department. When we modeled the work groups in each department, and attached jobs to process steps, it became clear that the job duties of the ODS for the department were actually limited to one activity: facilitating meetings and training sessions. In the corporate-wide department, the ODS could be attached to any number of different projects, and the role included gathering and analyzing needs and determining the solution...and perhaps facilitating along the way.

Special Note: Although jobs can be attached to work group models to clarify role relationships, it is best to model the whole organization in a certain order. This book in the Work Trilogy series—designed to clarify and improve your work as a manager—assumes you are not involved in organizing the business as implicit in *The Business Model* of the Language of Work. There is a logical, preferred order to modeling and aligning work for the entire enterprise: first business unit modeling, followed by core process, job, and finally work group modeling. Identifying jobs such as shown above would be done to core process models. However, the reality is that modeling jobs or the work group often occurs first; this is still a powerful approach, even in its standalone form.

Conducting Meetings

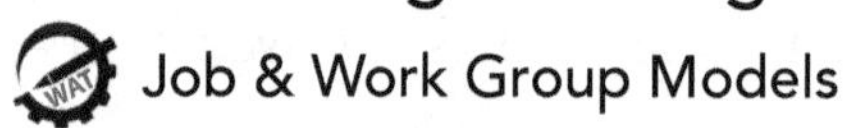

One of your most time-consuming roles as a manager is that of conducting meetings. It is here that everyone on your team gets to see you in action and judge, in particular, your leadership, organizational, and communication skills. It is our experience that entirely too many meetings in organizations are full of surprises. We recognize that electronic tools have helped to reduce this chaos, but we find that even the most structured meetings can end up being random and un-productive at identifying solutions to work issues. If a manager, on the other hand, were to structure most work meetings on use of the related Language of Work Models, you would find that such meetings will be greatly enhanced. By structuring meetings on a common understanding of the work and how it is best achieved, everyone knows where the discussion is going and how to contribute. Thus, in a work group discussion, use a work group model. In a job role discussion, use job models, and if an executive use core process and business unit models.

The Work Formula, as we have already noted, displays the Effect and then the Cause of work: It shows the systemic relationship between Outputs/Consequences relative to Inputs, Conditions, Process Steps, and Feedback. In this regard, a manager recently introduced to the use of the Language of Work, noted its value for meeting structure and follow-up:

> *"I've been building an ops manual, SOPs, and project management tools for my company based on your work formula/ language. It has revolutionized our way of defining processes. One of the reasons I love it is because it overlays on a macro scale as well as a micro level. By micro I mean I've made meeting minute templates that define action items for tasks as well as the conditions, inputs needed, and feedback for the action item output. Maybe I went a little wild applying it, but it's been working great."*

Meetings structured on this basis are focused discussions on how to make work more efficient and effective. Thus, while each job holder and team member reports on results (outputs and consequences), the meeting also explores the processes used and any obstacles that prevent achievement. As each person contributes to the status on any project—itself structured on the LoW—each person can easily attend to what is being said and comment or suggest improvements based on inputs, conditions, process steps, and feedback. Any related work issues of work support, standards, HR, or financial support can also be addressed coherently and in context of how they positively or negatively impact work execution. Comments and issues are no longer just that, but relevant in the context of improving work implementation.

Team meetings that jump from one topic or issue to another, without resolution, lead to much more confusion and stress than necessary. The LoW simply makes being together-as-one possible; therefore your meeting structure should be well organized, known, and conducted. Here are some useful guidelines for structuring your meetings:

- Identify first what consequences and outputs need addressing (in work group and/or job models).
- Identify the focus of reporting or discussing: process steps, inputs, conditions, feedback, and/or work support.
- Identify who will cover each aspect.
- Identify desired changes, if any: Who will make the change and when? Does a model need to be developed or updated to assure success?
- What are the milestones? Do any dates need to be changed?
- What are the next steps? What feedback is needed, and to whom? When will the next meeting take place?

Improving Quality

There should be an inextricable link between improving quality and continuous improvement. And, rather than viewing this as a program to be added to your managing function, as is the case in most organizations, the Language of Work Model embodies quality improvements as a natural extension of work understanding and implementation. For details, see Chapter 9.

Problem Solving

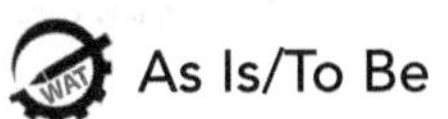

Problem solving has often been an elusive skill. It seems to require a creative side that we may think we or others don't possess. The reality is, however, that problem solving is largely a matter of getting clarity first about the problem and then being able to think creatively about how to solve or resolve it. In fact, it's almost impossible to achieve the solution without the clarity. That is where the Work Formula comes in. The formula is largely about achieving work clarity and with such then comes the power to say, "This is what I would do!" Let's see an example.

An organization provided in-home nursing and personal care to residents in three counties (Divisions 1, 2, and 3).The newly hired director had heard about problems from board members, employees, and clients. Various people offered solutions. What the client needed was an easy way to display the current reality (AS IS) and the desired reality (TO BE), in order to develop a series of solutions and obtain board approval. By using the LoW AS IS/TO BE WAT, all the observations of the various groups could be laid out in a clear, logical, and un-emotional way. An example of this is shown in Figure 31.

In the figure, problem solving is organized in terms of the six elements of the Work Formula for both AS IS and TO BE. Once the director of this organization, with input from the employees, had laid out the current state of the agency (AS IS), it was possible to describe what should be in place. This became the TO BE state.

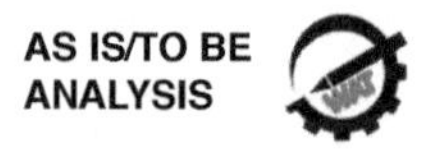

PROJECT: In-Home Nursing and Personal Care

	INPUTS	CONDITIONS	PROCESS STEPS	OUTPUTS	CONSEQUENCES	FEEDBACK
AS IS	• Staffing is inadequate in Division • Recruiting & retaining employees difficult • No Mgmt. presence in Division 2 • No Mgmt. present in Division 3	• Funding is limited • Benefits not provided to field staff • BOD does not see funding as its mission • No policy to call-outs • Cost overruns	• Training of field staff is minimal • Inefficiencies slowing work • Duplicate computer systems • Orientation too broad • Limited HR support at Div. 2 &3	• Services offered are limited	• Current reputation is poor • Teamwork is weak • Public unaware of services • Funding is inadequate	• Communication between offices is weak • Recognition of staff is needed
TO BE	• Staffing is good • Employee turnover is low	• Budget is balanced • Filed staff get paid vacation & group health access • Board is high functioning • Callouts are minimal • Client changes are controlled	• Field staff well trained • Work is efficient • Systems support works • HR Support works	• New Services successfully added quarterly	• Reputation is great • Team is strong • Public awareness is high	• Communication flows in all directions • Staff feels treasured

Figure 31

The third step was to then determine what to do for each gap between the AS IS and the TO BE. This should be done in a logical way—addressing the easiest first and moving on to the more difficult. In addition, research might be needed to find Best Practices, and that research might include consultation with experts in the problem at hand.

Following the 80/20 rule, 80% of problems can be resolved once the problem is agreed on by all parties.

As a final consideration in using AS IS/TO BE for problem solving, a more granular version of this that the authors have devised and used with great success is represented in Figure 32.

AS IS/TO BE PROBLEM SOLVING:

GAPS, CHANGE STATEMENTS, INTERVENTION OPTIONS & SELECTION	INPUT	CONDITIONS	PROCESS	FEEDBACK
GAP — AS IS				
GAP — TO BE				
CHANGE Is	☐ Establish ☐ Improve ☐ Maintain ☐ Extinguish	☐ Establish ☐ Improve ☐ Maintain ☐ Extinguish	☐ Establish ☐ Improve ☐ Maintain ☐ Extinguish	☐ Establish ☐ Improve ☐ Maintain ☐ Extinguish
CHANGE STATEMENT				
INTERVENTION OPTIONS				
INTERVENTIONS TO BE USED				

(page _ of _)

Figure 32

This version of problem solving is useful where a more detailed analysis is needed to get at the various root aspects of the problem being analyzed. The author (Langdon, 2001) developed some years ago an alternative to root cause analysis called the "Change of State Analysis." That source provides a reading on this tool that further explains the analysis and it is mentioned here as a useful alternative for your consideration as a manager when doing problem solving with your team. Its chief benefit is that it helps those analyzing the problem see what specific factors need to change and how so that appropriate solutions are easier to determine in combination with one another, since problems are often not solved by a single solution, but rather by a combination of interventions/actions/means.

Resolving Conflict

Resolving conflicts is an uncomfortable role for most managers. No one likes to be seemingly put in the position of a bad guy, but dealing effectively with conflict also demonstrates that you are a competent and fair manager. The LoW helps you have confidence in your ability to resolve conflicts.

Conflicts in the workplace are usually of two kinds: personal issues or work issues. Much has been written about handing personal issues—in fact, sometimes one would think the workplace was a hotbed of alienation and dysfunction. All the personality tools, from the DIRT index, through Meyers-Briggs and even the enneagram, are touted to provide an understanding of human differences in order to reduce conflicts.

All of that is well and good. There is certainly a place for such psychological approaches, but remember rarely is a manager well trained or certified in resolving issues created by personal agendas, personality differences, deep-seated biases, or even outside relationships.

Most—if not all—the conflicts that arise because of the work (the second cause) can be resolved by using the Language of Work. This is chiefly achieved by having discussions that center on the execution of individual or collective work using appropriate job and/or work group models that keep resolutions focused on the work rather than on the personalities.

Once a problem has been identified and agreed on, the cause or causes can also be identified. Gone are the blame and the emotion associated with work problems. Pinpointing the source of the problem on a black-and-white model allows parties to generate solutions. Is this a problem in quantity? Quality? Timeliness? Process? Then a solution can be generated as a team: changes of resources, changes in policy or procedure, discussions among managers, etc.

A feature of the Language of Work Formula that makes conflict resolution so effective is that the emotional component of such discussions can be reduced or eliminated. When the conflict in work execution is framed in less personal terms, the path to solutions become more obvious and the focus is consistently on the work and making it better, not on complaints, blame, or individual personalities.

Understand that conflict can also be related to work support issues (i.e., why the company isn't providing safety training, for example). We have found that such support issues need to be linked to work execution. The LoW provides explicit definitions of both work execution (models) and support (matrices) to keep conflict resolution centered on the issues at hand, and again not on the personal, emotional feelings. How these work support, human relations, and financial issues are best addressed is covered elsewhere in this and the two other books of *The Work Trilogy*.

Measuring Work

Work Formula

Measuring work in business has most often taken the form of, "What should we measure?" rather than really discovering what requires measuring. This guessing at what to measure stems primarily from there not being, until now, a complete and definitive definition of what constitutes work. We know we are able, through business, core processes, job, and work group models, (and work standards, work support, HR, and financial support) to identify what specifically can and should be measured. In essence, what was traditionally a guessing game or one aimed at measuring only financial considerations, has become knowing specifically what should be measured in terms of the Work Formula.

Since you have already learned that the Language of Work Model is a behavioral cause and effect definition of work that shows the relationship between what is produced (outputs and consequences) by the interaction of inputs, conditions, process steps, and feedback, it therefore becomes very clear in any given work group or job model what needs to be measured. Thus, we begin with measuring if the consequences and their related outputs have been achieved. If not, what should be measured as contributing to the failure to achieve? The six elements are the beginning point of what needs measurement as far as work goes. It is to be noted, in the case of job models, that you may want to also measure the skills and knowledge components that are specified, as well the presence of attributes, the attainment of competencies, and the like.

Finally, in the broader view of work as defined in the LoW, there are additional factors influencing work attainment that may need to be measured. For example, we might want to measure the many aspects of Work Support. As is noted later, in the chapter on continuous improvement, one way to measure work support is by soliciting and noting concerns expressed by employees on an ongoing basis.

Your part in this as a manager is fundamentally to know what to measure relative to individual job models and your team (work group model). This can be made clear by using the LoW.

Transferring Knowledge

Job & Work Group Models

Every day there is the possibility that you will need to transfer knowledge about some aspect of work. It could be because one of your workers is going on vacation, or you have a short-term health problem on your staff, one of the workers is being promoted, or for any other reasons you need to train or orient a new worker to his or her job and your team. Then there are bigger reasons, of course, for knowledge transfer, including retirement, change of job, or a merger or acquisition that changes who does the work that others have done. Knowledge transfer has increasingly become crucial to maintaining business success as aging workers retire. Models can play a key role in knowledge transfer. We suggest two ways this can be done.

First, job models serve, as has already been noted, as an orientation tool: They provide the big picture of individual work. By starting with the deliverables and the consequences, one can explain to another person the what (outputs) and the why (consequences) of the job. Individual employees can be encouraged to resist the temptation to make random observations about their work—including favorite gripes, war stories, or the truncated bits and pieces that are commonly referred to as the fire hose approach. Instead, after providing the big picture, you can get a holder of a job to focus on the next two critical elements: the inputs and the conditions. Here, employees tell where to find the various inputs, make observations about the timeliness of receipt, discuss the dynamics of the white space between departments, address triggers, and in general flesh out the picture of what they use and where it comes from. By covering the conditions, they can save the new person embarrassment or even punishment. (Things that seem logical may be against the law—so Employee Handbooks and HR rules are really helpful, especially to new workers. And the unwritten rules that govern culture can be landmines for those new to the organization.) Feedback sources are useful as well, in finding out if a mid-course correction is needed, and when a job is considered complete.

Once these elements have been recorded, the process steps can be discussed. Often there is more detail in these steps than a person can absorb easily, but providing any job aids, checklists, worksheets, sample work, historical resources—and linking them to the precise processes that they are used for—provides a long-lasting aid to the person who will be receiving the knowledge.

And, of course, a knowledge transfer should include important considerations specified in a job model when it comes to skills and knowledge (and where to acquire them, if necessary). There could be a description of work standards, available work support resources, relevant human relations considerations implicit in the job, and financial sources and other pertinent information about the job.

A second way to transfer knowledge is by capturing the general knowledge and artifacts that make up the job. This often takes the form of recording with the "retiree" the nature and scope of the job. A recorded electronic interview centered against the backdrop of the job model allows the individual to describe and demonstrate how the work was/is done. Thus, the present holder of the job fills in this template (of course with more detail): "My job involves producing these products and services. I use these resources and attend to these rules. I have figured out the following good ways of doing the job with others and my customers. And, I always let my manager know when and how I need help." As is often the case, individuals have devised special forms and tools to aid them in doing their work over the years, and these need to be captured as knowledge to be passed on to others now and in the future. People who have been on the job for decades have often become unconsciously competent, meaning they do not remember that they never knew something. For a novice, this is very frustrating. Using a job model allows the knowledge to be transferred in a much more systematic and thorough way.

Reviewing Performance

Have you ever…

- needed a meaningful way to talk about how to improve an employee's work?
- been frustrated by needing to measure personality traits ("gets along well with others") more than real performance ("meets deadlines with superior product")?
- left a performance review without a plan to make work better?
- floundered in telling an employee how their performance failed to meet expectations?

Everybody, especially managers, seems to hate performance reviews. Managers feel they don't do them well: They see them as a time-consuming, futile exercise, handed down from management, and that puts them in an awkward position with their work force. Furthermore, few of us want to be judged, so we may not like judging.

Employees generally both hate and desire reviews. Again, no one likes to be judged. No one likes to get a traffic ticket. And most performance reviews don't provide any tangible feedback that can be used to make the next year more satisfying than the last year. Still, we would like to improve and seek help that truly helps.

Everyone (managers, employees, and HR staff) is so mystified by the process that organizations often substitute long forms for good ones; try to separate performance review from compensation adjustment; finally try to engage everyone in the process by creating 360^0 as if performance were a popularity contest. The problem is not that the idea of performance review (appraisal, assessment, etc.) is a bad idea, but rather that no one knows exactly what to review. There is fundamental lack of understanding about what performance (that is, work) is and how people should talk about it. Given such, enterprises often abandon the practice all together.

Another set of forms with questions about attitudes will not solve the problem. New compensation strategies, no matter how cool, will not meet the need, nor make the manager or worker feel any better. Performance reviews are not an exercise in filling out forms, but rather a simple discussion about the work one has done, what was well done, and what needs improving over the next year.

In the Language of Work Model, your performance review with a worker should be viewed and executed in an *effect* and *cause* relationship. Periodically—at least twice a year and preferably on an ongoing basis—the manager needs to review the "effects" a worker is achieving. Using a job model to guide such a performance review, the manager and worker first review the outputs and consequences—the combined *effect*—of work. If either outputs and/or consequences are not being achieved, there is likely a set of *causes* that led to this. These causes are rooted in the other, articulated elements of the work that is specified in the job model. Thus, the manager and employee can review—as a beginning point—the inputs, conditions, process steps, and/or feedback to identify the root cause of the performance misfire.

In behavioral terms, work is a cause and effect relationship. Thus:

CAUSE

- Process Steps
- Inputs
- Conditions
- Feedback

EFFECT

- Outputs
- Consequences

The following summarizes some of the root causes which might be responsible for failing to achieve outputs and consequences:

1. Were the process steps not followed? Were they not completed? Or done poorly?

2. Were there inputs that were not utilized, came late, or were of poor quality?
3. Were there conditions not followed? Or did the conditions serve as obstacles to completing the work?
4. Was feedback missing that might have helped make corrections before they went wrong? Or was reinforcement missing?
5. Did the organization fail to provide appropriate or needed work support? (Example: a poorly designed work space or lack of lighting.)
6. Were underlying skill, knowledge, or attributes lacking?

As the causes are analyzed in a discussion between you and the employee, emphasis can be on analysis of work achievement, what worked well and what needs fixing. The question is not one of placing blame, but what has been done well, and what can be done better in the future and how. Since the Job Model provides skills and knowledge related to inputs, conditions, process steps, and feedback, these can be explored in fundamental ways to enhance performance.

It is recommended that the results of this discussion be given to HR so that they can develop remediation strategies and resources across the organization, such as training and other performance improvement interventions.

Perhaps the strongest advantage of this approach is that the two parties can work together to achieve a common goal: great performance. The performance review system (Language of Work) helps to keep the conversation nonjudgmental and focused on the elements of work.

Career Development

Many workers have hopes for work that is more interesting, challenging, and/or lucrative—beyond what they are currently doing. We recognize that working a lifetime in any single job may be fulfilling for some, but others will leave if they cannot grow within an organization. So organizations miss out when they do not nurture the dreams and expectations of their employees.

The consequences are not just lack of employee engagement or low morale; there are substantial costs involved in recruiting and training new employees which can be contained with a strong commitment to career development.

At the same time, we must recognize that organizations may not have the brilliance—or the resources—to develop robust talent management or career development programs. And those that are developed might be designed for "High Pots" (employees considered to have high potential), or executives-in-training, or other groups deemed critical by the enterprise.

In its simple form, when job models are visible (transparent) to all, career development is an easy process. Individuals can identify jobs or even select parts of jobs they are interested in, review the requirements clearly delineated in these models, and negotiate terms for learning, practicing, and achieving. This process serves as a self-selection tool, eliminating the glamorous jobs with outputs too difficult or uninteresting to pursue.

By homing in on desirable jobs, employees can select outputs of jobs they are interested in and establish mentoring relationships with holders of those jobs to learn new skills. For example, a junior accountant can establish an agreement with a senior accountant to learn given outputs. A mentoring arrangement is established between the two parties and supported by you as a manager. The role of manager is to encourage, support, and assure resources, time, and any direct assistance (e.g., job/task shadowing) to their joint effort. This becomes an informal career development opportunity. With thought, it can also provide a cross-job backup system that could prove vital in times of increasing job demands, changes, illnesses, and the like.

For example, one of the authors realized that work in a similar but different department was intriguing: transactional HR instead of strategic HR. It was a tool she needed to put into her quiver if she was to be a candidate for an HR director job. She identified one of the outputs from the Job Model (Employees Hired) and requested that her director give her a one-week job-shadowing gig. Once successful in this endeavor, she went on to participate in a compensation review, and eventually to be given full transactional HR authority for a small department.

One can easily see that job models can make career development more worker-initiated, thus more likely to occur and be satisfactory when actively supported by management. When linked to a career path system supported and established by the company through HR, job models play an even greater role. But lacking such sophistication, even small units can provide career resilience—through job models—to all employees. And armed with a job model, it is possible for any individual to develop, clearly and systematically, an entire career.

Implementing Other Work Functions Using the Work Formula

You have by now gleaned the versatility of the Work Formula and associated use of Work Analytic Tools in implementing numerous management functions. The LoW Managing Model can enhance the way you presently perform management functions. Because the Work Formula is an operational definition of work, it can be applied to nearly everything in business, big or small—because business is all about work and the LoW is the definition of work.

Faced with any of the myriad challenges of your working day, you can use the Work Formula yourself or with others to think of ways to plan, implement, and measure work. It thus becomes a way of thinking and operating; it is a systematic way of thinking. It is a *Language of Work*. You will plan, discuss, implement, measure, reinforce, and correct work—all applying the universal Work Formula.

Here are four questions that you can answer when applying the Work Formula to *any* aspect of work:

1. How will the six elements of work interact when I implement the function?
2. How do I assure that my workforce is involved as much as feasible so as to gain their insights *and* their commitment?
3. What elements will I measure/observe to know that a function has worked, or make necessary adjustments to make it work?

4. What things do I, as the manager, need to do to support creating a healthy work environment?

Chapter 8

How Do I Develop Work Models with My Department?

> You understand the need to model your department, but should you do it yourself or with others? Are there perhaps internal or external resources that could assist?

You should not model the work group solely on your own (although you could), because not involving others in your group means you will miss out on some very valuable input, let alone consensus and commitment. The same is true of developing job models. Proceeding without your group's involvement means you will miss the workforce's perception of the work and their commitment to doing it right. You will also miss out on other valuable data as to ways the team effort could be better supported. We therefore suggest a team approach to work modeling to assure clear and open communication with and by others. This doesn't mean everyone has to be involved in the initial modeling, but everyone needs to review and offer any missing input on the initial and final drafts of any work model. We'll show you how this is done.

You basically have four options for modeling the work group, jobs, and needed work support:

1. Model everything yourself with your team.
2. Use a skilled facilitator with yourself and the team.
3. Use someone certified in the Language of Work.
4. Use our online modeling service.

There are, of course, relative advantages to each of these options and we will describe them so you can decide what will work best for you and your team.

Model Everything Yourself with Your Team

Managers come in two basic forms: those who see the world as nuts and bolts, a kind of engineering approach to things; and those who are more holistic, creative, and highly people-oriented. Neither way is better than the other, but since the Language of Work is a systems approach, it may appeal initially more to the nuts-and-bolts people. On the other hand, the more holistic folks may find this way of looking at work helps them clarify issues and communicate more clearly. If you are comfortable with the idea of modeling, you might facilitate it yourself.

If you decide to do it yourself, then you should utilize the 5-7 key individuals in your department (or everyone, if yours is a department of fewer than 8 people). The modeling of a work group and jobs is not just about the work models you produce, but the way the content is built through the eyes of all involved parties. Managers have told us numerous times that they had no idea their people saw certain aspects of their work the way they did. But this is only one thing that can occur. What is particularly valuable in involving your team is that the modeling process results in clarity, consensus-building and some improvement of work processes. By modeling with the team, you are establishing a common view of the work, aimed at specific, agreed-upon outcomes (outputs and consequences). You will also see their views of the problems that exist and need to be addressed. With such clarity, you will be amazed at the answers they arrive at. And you'll find an added commitment to doing what it takes to improve things. Doing the modeling on your own, without the team, will not get you these benefits.

Use a Skilled Facilitator

Generally, we recommend use of a skilled facilitator, either because this kind of facilitation is not in your skillset, and/or because as the manager, you will learn far more by participating rather than leading. Because the focus of the discussion is on filling in the boxes (i.e., elements of the Work Formula), knowledge—not power—is key. The system itself tends to be self-correcting, so people learn if they place elements in the wrong boxes.

You can utilize either an internal or external facilitator. Provided they have read about and understood the preferred order of modeling the six work elements, they should be able to guide you and your team through the requirements outlined in this book.

Use Someone Certified in The Language of Work

There are people who have been certified in the Language of Work and have employed it in a variety of enterprise settings. They know the modeling process at various levels of work and the challenges of different work models. They are proficient and thus save time in modeling. You may contact Performance International for the name of a certified facilitator.

Use Our Online Modeling Service

The authors and our associates offer online modeling, producing an effective result without our being onsite. Using such services as Go-to-Meeting or other web-based meeting services, we have found that online modeling works very well. Besides the obvious advantage of utilizing your internal work experts, who may be widely distributed, we have found that online modeling focuses everyone's attention on the task very well. What it doesn't offer, of course, is the ability to see body language, facial expressions, and nonverbal cues during the modeling. Some of the team-building that can occur face to face is harder to create as well, unless the members of the team already know each other. Still, online modeling is effective and can be most useful when you want to save on development costs. Contact us at Performance International.

We will conclude this chapter by offering some other general guidelines to make your modeling experience successful. We will repeat some we have already mentioned for emphasis and add others.

1. While the best modeling sessions have 5-7 participants, it is critical to use your entire team in the modeling process to build understanding, consensus, and commitment. While only some of your staff can be used in the actual modeling sessions, which are best when kept small, everyone else should be encouraged to review, validate, and provide

their input to what has been produced. Models are always "working documents" that continue to change as necessary.

2. Think about the benefit of utilizing others who make or provide inputs to your department. These are other groups you relate to in the chain of work, technical consultants, and the like. They may have valuable insights about their challenges in giving you what you want and need. Their perspective can be important if you use it for input to what you have/will model.
3. Think about the benefit of utilizing an (internal or external) customer or client in your modeling. Additional perspective is critical to your success, since clients are the reason you are doing the work. As one of the principles of Kaizan suggests, if you want quality input, it's best to go and insist on it rather than waiting to see what you get.
4. Make sure to model the work elements in the order we have specified and tested over the years: outputs, inputs, conditions, consequences, process steps, and finally feedback. Figure 5 (10-Minute Teach job aid) is an excellent modeling aid to have in front of everyone as work is being modeled. Also make use of the 10-Minute Teach online at https://youtu.be/Nn7tLm4nRLU

Chapter 9

Achieving Continuous Improvement

Any manager who wants to run a really effective department knows he or she must continuously improve: improve productivity and results, reduce costs, improve timeliness and customer service, and provide greater quantities while improving the quality of products. Continuous improvement on all these fronts can be overwhelming.

We conclude *The Managing Model* with what it takes to continually assure your department is efficient and effective. We explore the importance of establishing a functional "mindset" that promotes continuous improvement from one's own initiative.

The leading attempts businesses have used to approach continuous improvement have been to install "programs." TQM, Lean Manufacturing, Quality Circles, Kaizan, and Agile are just some of the popular approaches to continuous improvement. These programs try to instill methods of improvement, while creating departments that encourage, reward, and indeed make such improvements.

The programs are add-ons to the current organization that, while often fairly effective, nonetheless suffer from a fatal flaw: Their very nature is an addition to the "regular" work. They are outside the way work is planned, organized, and implemented and cannot totally affect the ongoing mind-set of the work force. They are, as such, seen as "what management wants me to do," rather than as "what I (we) might naturally do if we only knew how and had the freedom to do so." If continuous improvement were a natural extension of work execution, then it follows that it would be more likely to occur on an ongoing basis compared to programs that often rise and ebb in direct relation to management interest and encouragement. Having said this, programmatic approaches can be useful, and it would be desirable to have improvement naturally occur as part of ongoing work implementation. We shall explain how the LoW can support programs as well as helping you develop and practice a mindset in improving your own work as a manager.

Note: Much of what we are about to describe for our "programmatic" approaches to continuous improvement has already been described in the content of certain management functions as part of the Manager/Worker Interface—see Figure 25. We won't repeat what has already been illustrated, but do want to further describe these functions as they relate to continuous improvement, including change management.

Enhancing Programmatic Continuous Improvement

There are three LoW tools that have proven worthy adjuncts to your existing programs for work improvement and change. These are described in the other two books of *The Work Trilogy* because executives and workers are also involved in them, but you have the chief accountability for improvements in your department.

These are:

- Performance Review/Appraisal Programs
- Dots on Models
- Cultural Audit and Worker Verbatims

Performance Review/Appraisal Programs

We covered the management function of performance reviews above, but now we will address the results of such reviews rather than the process of completing them.

The organizational challenge in building continuous improvement is reliable and situationally accurate information that would actually impact work, morale, and profit significantly. This data needs to lead to improvements in all aspects of work execution. Additionally, the change needs to improve work support as well (our layers of work standards, work support, HR, and financial support). A culture in which managers are not deeply knowledgeable about the work contributes to this problem. When performance appraisals are based on attitudes and the ability to "play well with others," they provide nothing useful for achieving continuous improvement. However, if done right—that is, based on the actual job deliverables and consequences—there is no better or more reliable source of data for continuous improvement. But doing it right is the key to the goal.

The LoW provides a relevant review of work for individuals or groups. The Job Model graphically displays the desired state of performance. Differences between the desired and the actual can be pinpointed. Articulating the gaps between them can be done mutually when performance review is a continuous improvement process and not a "gotcha game." Once the gaps have been identified, they can be linked to problems with inputs, conditions, process, or feedback. Parsing the individual data results in a series of interventions which might include making inputs available on a timelier basis, changing conditions so that deadlines are reasonably determined, making actual processes more foolproof, or developing more effective communications systems.

These are changes made based on data collected from individual performance reviews and offer the opportunity for continuous improvement to the individual. However, the LoW's greatest power lies in the fact that the paradigm for work review is the same as that for modeling the work. The same six-element Work Formula used to create the Job Model is turned on itself to review the job performance, this time in an effect and cause relationship. In addition, whole work groups, core processes, and business units can also be defined the same way. This provides opportunities for organization-wide data collection and analysis leading to significant improvements. As the authors suggest in other sources, this can become a system-wide dashboard for optimizing work—see http://www.youtube.com/watch?v=WhS2KMdHm70

The systemic (behavioral) grounding of the Work Formula not only defines work, but simultaneously determines the appropriate places for measuring that work. It follows that the performance review can reveal areas of needed improvement. If that information is acted upon, you, as the manager, in cooperation with the worker(s), can create continuous and timely improvements. When individual data is collected and aggregated, analysis will show where the whole organization needs to make improvements. When that information is relayed to internal entities such as HR, training, organizational effectiveness, and programmatic entities (e.g., quality circles), the data can serve to foster improvements system-wide. The whole organization can rise in work effectiveness and efficiency. Even if you choose not to provide the information (or such entities do not exist), you will foster departmental or team improvements that are likely to get noticed. And at a minimum, your own skills as a manager will be enhanced.

Dots on Models

The quality movement of decades ago introduced the use of dots to display various notions. The display of dots was a way to capture the implicit thinking of the members of a group and could be also used for tentative votes or to eliminate areas of potential discussion without a lot of distracting debate. Managers can use it effectively in improving work groups/teams.

An example from our consultancy practice clearly illustrates how you can focus discussion on your work group model.

Dots on Models works because it assumes that those closest to the work—the workers—know where the problems are and possess answers to most performance issues. Unfortunately, employees often suffer in identifying, proposing, and implementing solutions because they do not have a good means to communicate their knowledge. Too often their views are assumed to be biased or short-sighted, only opinions equal to anyone else's. The Language of Work resolves that issue. Because the work is described by building models at the four levels of work, solutions are always grounded in the clear, consensus-driven definition of work, which makes it easy to identify and prioritize problems, encourages collaboration in solving them, and ensures commit to implementation. Since the entire process is driven by those who are experiencing the problem(s), the results are desirable, achievable, and grounded in the work. Management is in the position of providing support, not direction.

Using Dots on Models is a tested process for identifying improvements in well-defined and understood work, leading to solutions committed to by those who have the problem/issue/opportunity. The way this tool works is to invite knowledgeable employees to identify where work could be improved. For a core process or work group model, such as the one illustrated in Figure 33, workers and managers are given a set of 15 colored adhesive dots to put onto a blown-up copy (3'x3' or 3'x4') of the model, using the dots to highlight work areas (inputs, conditions, process steps, feedback) they deem in need of improvement. They may distribute their dots singly, in groups, or all in one place.

The result is a visual picture into the minds of all participants, indicating what they–as a group—see as the most significant areas needing improvement. This is highly efficient, taking at most 15 minutes. Follow-up discussion is then concentrated on answering questions about why people dotted the elements they

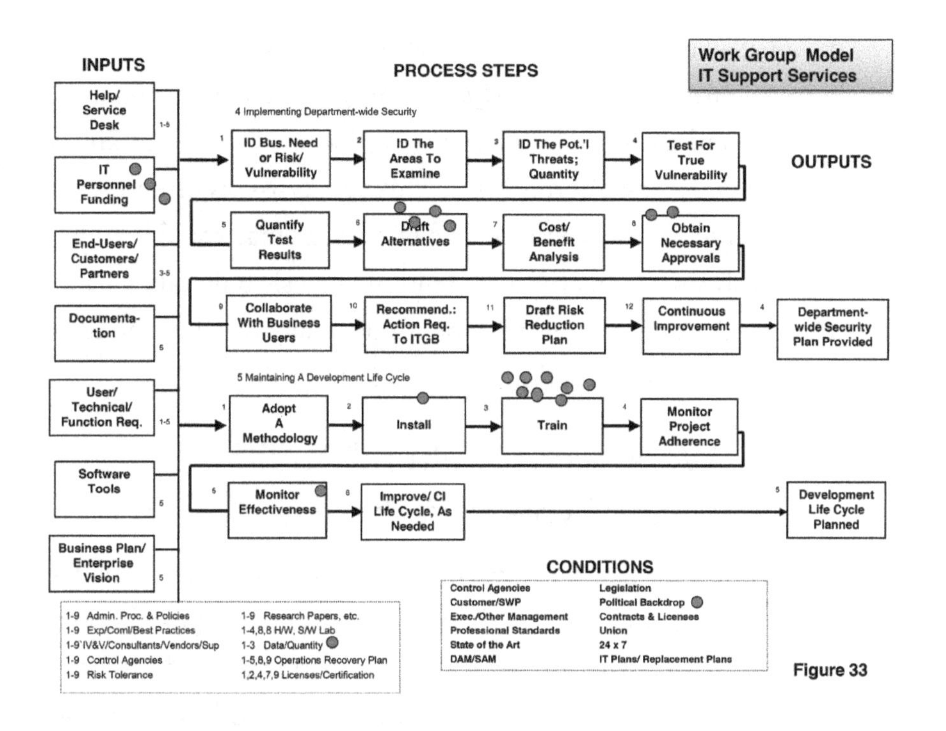

Figure 33

did, rank-ordering priorities, identifying potential solutions, and getting clarity on the results of this process. Consensus is built with a facilitator, leading to areas that participants are committed to finding and implementing solutions for.

For example, Figure 33, step 6 of process 4 and step 3 of process 5, as well as an input related to IT Personnel Funding, received the largest number of dots. Everyone has a chance to see what is in the minds of their fellow team members. The facilitator of this activity will ask what issues led to the individual dots. The group can decide if these items are outliers, or if more attention from the group should be paid. This eliminates passionate arguments about nonessential issues, while giving the "voters" a chance to explain their use of a dot on any given issue.

A full discussion then follows as to the nature of the work challenges, their causes (perhaps doing root cause analysis, if needed), and potential solutions. A change of state analysis (Langdon, 2003)—an alternative to cause analysis—is often useful in rendering how work would be changing and what could be done to accomplish the change(s). This kind of analysis only takes 10 or 15 minutes. Dots on Models may be used for any or all of the four levels of work encompassed in the Language of Work Model.

Work Scans: Cultural Audits and Worker Verbatims

As the manager of your department, one of your major obligations is to continually improve the work environment (also known as "the culture") so that work execution is as effective and efficient as possible. Using job models and work group models based on the LoW provides a foundation for making such improvements. But we have argued that managing work execution is not enough; work must also be supported by the organization. The essence of the managerial and executive roles is creating a work environment that presents the fewest possible obstacles to work completion. By addressing work support, you are enhancing the ability of workers to accomplish the tasks in their job and work group models.

The challenge, however, is how to do this effectively and well. Perhaps you have been promoted into your position and remember the frustrations you experienced on the line. These you can readily address. Perhaps you have a good lieutenant who fills you in on where improvements are needed. Perhaps you have a "vociferous laggard"—a complainer who lets you know what needs to be addressed. Or you have done all of these—or none of them—and are looking for a more effective method of identifying obstacles to employee performance. The LoW's Work Support Matrix (introduced in Chapter 6) can be used in at least two ways to improve the culture of the organization. (Many behavioral psychologists have examined culture over the years. This matrix is based on their work, which we then compiled using the Language of Work Formula).

There are two principal ways to use the Work Support Matrix to identify and improve the environment in which you and your team work:

- the Cultural Audit
- the Worker Verbatims

Cultural Audit

A cultural audit helps you to measure the degree of work support currently provided. You might think of this as a kind of "dashboard" for work support. As with the dashboard of a car or airplane, there are numerous indicators (fuel, oil, speed, etc.) that you observe and to which you make adjustments as you drive. To address work support, you'll need a clear sense of what to look for and assess. The Work Support Matrix can be the dashboard you need for organizational health; it provides the indicators you may have intuited or heard about and assembles them is a systematic way.

At its simplest, a cultural audit involves reviewing the content of the boxes at the business unit, core process, job, or work group levels and comparing workforce assessment against these items. Input can come one-on-one where you chat with or interview employees and compare their issues with items in the matrix or can be gathered in tweets at #whatcanwedotoimprove?, in all hands meetings or in any way, as long as it is aimed at the content of the matrix. The essential thing is that you are measuring the current state against the standard (in the matrix) and you'll be determining what work support needs to be established, improved, maintained, or eliminated.

For example, you might sit down with employees to review each indicator in the matrix. Together you evaluate the adequacy of that support item, noting what needs to be changed. If the matrix indicates that job descriptions are important in supporting employees, this would trigger a discussion on the adequacy of current job descriptions. Once the discussion is complete, you would know whether job descriptions are adequate or need improvement. If the latter, you would know that HR needs to make changes. You could ask whether a Job Model would improve clarity, whether the kind of performance review methodology suggested in the LoW would work better than job descriptions, whether technology would affect the work, and so on. In this way, you could be moving from generalized complaints to proactive continuous improvement for your employees.

Another way to audit your work group is to develop a survey with specific questions seeking areas for improvement. For example:

> "Do you feel the level of feedback from your manager is adequate?"
> "How could we improve client input to us?"

Any of these general questions could be drilled down to more specific indicators as shown in the Support Matrix. If you have been unhappy, or otherwise reluctant, to use a survey, you will be pleased with how using the LoW Work Support Matrix will help improve both the development and results. Based on the factors that make for efficiencies in the organization, such audit questions are targeted to the work execution that they align to. When the surveys are followed through on by management, employees are pleased as well because the results relate to their work, and continuous improvement is achieved. Such positive reinforcement helps foster a positive work environment.

By way of an example, Figure 34 (Work Support Matrix) shows a convenient way to summarize improvements needed at the job level. The highlights capture the results of an audit with employees.

	INPUTS	*CONDITIONS*	*PROCESS STEPS*	*OUTPUTS*	*CONSEQUENCES*	*FEEDBACK*
JOB LEVEL	CLIENT NEEDS & RESOURCES	WORK INFLUENCES	WORK METHODS	JOB DELIVERABLES	INDIVIDUAL RESULTS	CONFIRMATIONS & SELF ADJUSTMENT
	Assignments	Attributes	Career Development Plan	Job Models	Customer Satisfaction	Dialogue
	Boss/Organization	Benefits/Pay	Documentation	Individual unit:	Job Satisfaction	Internal Client Evaluations
	Equipment/Facilities	Budget	Performance Improve-	• Knowledge	Personal Satisfaction	Performance Appraisal
	Goals & Objectives	Ergonomics	ment Interventions	• Products	Tie to Work Group	Rewards & Recognition
	Job Description	Employee	Skill Maint./Devel.	• Services		Turnover
	Identified Client Needs	Handbook	Succession Planning			
	Strategy	Ethics	Work Flow			
		Policies	Work Tools			
		Safety				
		Schedule				
		Workload				

Figure 34

This example shows that employees were often confused about the goals and objectives. They also did not understand client needs. Both inputs needed managerial attention. The manager in this example also had heard requests for better work benches (Ergonomics) and safety glasses (conditions), but had initially thought that complainers were just griping. Having talked with the employees about this, she now saw the relationship between these requests and the conditions that influenced the speed of production and the absentee rate. Employees also pointed out that if they knew there was a job to be had beyond the one they were in (part of Process Steps), they would see a future with the company, so succession planning made the list. Since succession is HR's purview, it was passed to them as a recommendation. Finally, the group identified the need for internal clients to evaluate their performance (feedback in the matrix) and in fact devised a quick sheet for getting that feedback.

Using the matrix in this way shows you are actively seeking and valuing your workers' input, while getting their buy-in to making improvements. You commit to making the improvements that you can and to escalate other discoveries, as appropriate. You will be demonstrating that you are proactive in making needed changes in the work environment with and for them as a team.

Worker Verbatims

Verbatims are another way to use the Work Support Matrix. They involve collecting worker comments organization-wide and tabulating the results against the Work Support Matrix. Rather than starting from the matrix to decide what to audit, employee data is collected in the employees' own words and matched to the matrix. This identifies gaps perceived by employees. It is differentiated from the organizational audit only by the way the information is gathered.

In this instance we are capitalizing on what employees are talking about as an indicator of what's wrong with the company. Every company is replete with employees expressing what the company isn't doing as well as it could. This is generally called "griping," "bitching," "rumor mongering," and "scuttlebutt." We call it "verbatims" to give it a more positive tone. These expressions should not be completely ignored, even though some may be disregarded because they have no value or are based on false information. However, as is more often the case, there are so many nuggets of useful information available that a method is needed for directly dealing with them. We propose a way that this can be done effectively.

Rather than beginning with the Work Support Matrix, and evaluating worker input against various elements, this scan begins free-form. Data can be obtained both formally and informally. Informally, one keeps an ear to the ground. Hearing comments, asking what the workers are thinking or feeling, learning what the scuttlebutt is and of course, today, what is being said on social media. Or perhaps use a "suggestion box," but find it ignored because rarely is anything done with the comments. Collect and write comments down as accurately as you can.

Alternatively, you can use a more formal approach. For example, you can elicit information following modeling or reviewing jobs (as in performance reviews) or after other work-focused meetings. Asking a question such as "What could the organization do (say, in terms a planned project) to help you get your work done?" or "How is the organization getting in the way of your work?" can provide relevant responses because the comments are in the context of a shared understanding of the work, as shown in the LoW models. Several examples of such verbatim comments are noted in Figure 35 from a session conducted by the authors.

JOB LEVEL WORKER SCAN VERBATIMS:

CLIENT NEEDS & RESOURCES (Inputs)
- There's too much work around here
- I wish I knew when there was a real emergency, and not just a loud customer complaining to the boss

WORK INFLUENCES (Conditions)
- Rules keep changing around here
- We need a template for our recommendations so we can compare ours to those of other analysts

WORK METHODS (Process Steps)
- Getting approvals requires too many dumb changes and revisions
- We need a quicker way to gather the AS-IS state data; couldn't the client do this?

CONFIRMATIONS & SELF ASSESSMENTS (Feedback)
- We have trouble getting data on System performance…it's like people don't trust us to look at it
- I wish the vendors did a better job of comparing us to other customers…they know a lot, but are afraid to tell us
- Our clients go to our boss instead of to us. We can do a quick fix a lot faster than waiting to hear from him.
- I would love to hear, "Good Job!" every once in a while.

Figure 35

Internal Client Evaluations.

As the *verbatim*—that is, word for word, without editing—comments are collected, they can be classified first under the major headings in the Work Support Matrix and then more granularly under the subheadings. Then, within these, the comments can be assigned to the subcategories that are linked to specific aspects of work support. In the example shown, we see a number of verbatim comments at the individual job level related to "Confirmations & Self-Assessments." These are attached specifically to the work support intervention called Internal Client Evaluations. When significant numbers of comments are found with a need to improve Internal Client Evaluations, it is highlighted on the matrix, with backup documentation included as needed. You can then tie the work support item directly to work execution in order to convince those in power that the workforce often has answers because they are so close to the work; thus these work scans provide a system for conveying to everyone the magnitude of the work support problems.

When all data from worker verbatims has been gathered and referenced to the specific interventions in the matrix, the frequency of such observations (as noted by the shaded area in Figure 35) helps prioritize needed changes. When you subsequently review the results with the workforce, they are quite astute in describing what interventions can be put in place, improved, and implemented to resolve these work support issues.

In summary, cultural audits and verbatims, summarized in the Work Support Matrix, provide a systematic way to account for and communicate useful recommendations for improvements both internally and to senior management. If you and others in charge follow up, you can go a long way toward developing and enhancing a healthy work environment.

As an ancillary note, whether instituting a cultural audit or worker Verbatims, we recommend that you work in concert with any available internal organizational effectiveness professionals. They generally are familiar with many of the services, programs, and other interventions found on the Work Support Matrix and can be useful in helping to collect, categorize, interpret data, and to find programs and services for continuous improvement.

Establishing a Mindset for Continuous Work Improvement

The very best way to continuously improve work occurs when the executives, managers, and workers set their individual minds and collective action toward improving work through their own initiative. Unfortunately, there are typically only a few individuals who make this a way of life in their careers. They constantly seek to learn new things, improve upon what they already know, get more education and training from the company, pursue a career path, want leadership roles, and participate in almost every opportunity to learn. Any company would love to hire and retain more such people. The problem is, continuous personal and career growth does not come naturally to most people.

The LoW, by clarifying work for everyone through the Work Formula, establishes a vocabulary for discussing work and making it better. The LoW is a version of systems thinking that helps to identify and meet work improvement opportunities. As a manager, you can capitalize on this vocabulary for improvement in your discussions, as well as prompting others to adopt it as well. As one manager recently put it, "As simple as it sounds, just using an active verb to make process statements helped my mental framework immensely." Here we will show you a few ways to promote systems thinking—a mindset for improvement.

In the early '90s we were just starting to introduce the use of LoW in several companies. Some early adopters of the LoW told us they still use it in some of the ways (e.g., modeling) we have introduced in this book. They also find the principles of the LoW embedded in their ongoing thinking, discussion, planning, measurement, and execution of work, including ongoing improvement. For example, meetings are often organized on what outputs and consequences are being addressed, followed by reporting, as needed, on actions concerning utilization of inputs, conditions, process steps, and/or feedback. Discussions are held on how the company can better support this work. Planning and problem- solving sessions follow a similar track. Many of these have been illustrated and described here in *The Managing Model,* connecting to the Manager/ Worker Interface. Several use the various kinds of Work Analytic Tools, and the Work Formula, in their daily actions. To our way of thinking, these uses demonstrate the power of systems thinking.

You can promote systems thinking implicit in the LoW Model—to establish a mindset—or culture—of continuous improvement. You can encourage your workers, for example, to report to you in Work Formula terms. You can ask them to analyze their own work, solve problems, and resolve work relationship issues using the Language of Work formula. Their descriptions will demonstrate a deeper knowledge of the system in which the problem or situation resides and often will offer the solution in its telling. Enhanced communication will reinforce the consistent use of this vocabulary, resulting in that systems thinking.

In addition to using the vocabulary of the Language of Work for thinking and communicating, there are two specific ways to build this mindset into your organization.

Workers and managers are encouraged to review the LoW-defined core processes, jobs, and work groups, using them to measure challenges and identify improvement needs. Those improvements can be made individually, in worker teams, or with management (using the LoW as a problem-solving technique). Here, too, the LoW provides and promotes a common, shared understanding of work that can be measured and continuously made better.

A more formal tool, as part of establishing the mindset, is a work analytic tool titled the Work Analysis Aid. It presents a series of questions we typically ask when helping organizations improve themselves. Our long use has internalized the questions so the process has become intuitive for us. We want the same thing to happen to you and your workforce—you ask the questions so automatically that they reflect a continuous improvement mindset.

As shown in Figures 36 and 37, the Work Analysis Aid is a list of probing questions about work execution (levels) and work support (layers). They lead to specific areas of needed improvement. Using this aid will help you think about cause and effect, resulting in systematic and systemic discussions about work. Continuous improvement can result quickly or be proposed to upper management for others whose purview it is, allowing you to be proactive.

Note that continuous improvement involves more than simply looking at the six elements of work. Work is affected by employees' skills and knowledge, entry- level proficiencies, and job attributes. Is there an entry-level skill you mistakenly assumed a worker possessed? Does a worker lack the skills needed to perform or a particular innate attribute for doing a specific job? These are aspects of continuous improvement that are critical for you, the manager,

Work Analysis Aid

Page 1 of 2

In General:
The Work Analysis Aid provides a systematic way to use work execution models and support matrices to review and decide needed change in work performance. Sample analysis questions—such as "What is the worth or value of an output?"—to the six elements and layers of work are provided to start your thinking as to how to resolve an identified work problem/need. Pose these questions after determining areas of work improvement from use of the Work Improvement Identification Aid.
You are reminded that there are four ways of changing work: (1) establish, (2) improve, (3) maintain, or (4) extinguish; keep such in mind when proposing work change. Questions are not limited to those listed here; they serve as a beginning to tailoring for your work environment.

WORK EXECUTION

A. First look at **Outputs** and **Consequences** for work results. Ask:
a) What is the worth (value) of each output to the customer/client?
b) Is the quality of this output sufficient for the next receiver to use well?
c) Is the quality in keeping with its cost?
d) Is it being done by the right person or unit?
e) Can it be transferred? Consolidated? Outsourced?
f) Can you reduce the frequency of the delivery of the output?
g) Can you reduce the number of people receiving the service?
Compare outputs to the consequences.
h) Are they aligned with each other?
i) Are any other new outputs needed to satisfy any of the identified consequences?

B. Look at **Conditions** for cause. Ask:
a) Are any of the conditions inhibiting successful performance of process steps, use of inputs, or feedback?
b) Do any conditions need to be modified?
c) Do any conditions need to eliminated?
d) Which of the conditions should be reinforced for adherence?
e) Could management do things to improve specific compliance? Or, remove debilitating conditions?

C. Look at **Process Steps** first for cause. Ask:
a) Where are the trouble spots in the process steps?
b) Who can address the trouble spots?
c) Are there "white spaces" that need to be better managed? (i.e., pass offs that "fall thru the cracks)
d) What skills and knowledge are needed to complete each step in the process? Which of these need to be further developed?
e) Is training effectively transferring to job? Would other interventions (i.e. mentoring) be more effective?
f) Can any of the steps be delegated?
g) Is the process being conducted by the right person or department?

WORK EXECUTION

Answers The Question:
"How are work problems to be resolved?

Figure 36

Work Analysis Aid

Page 2 of 2

WORK EXECUTION

D. Look at **Inputs** for cause. Ask:
a) Is the quality of this input sufficient to the do-er?
b) What form does the input come in? Can the input be systematized? Automated? Organized differently? Consolidated? Do you wait for or go get the output?
c) Is the input being received by the right person or unit?
d) Can the waiting time be changed? Reduced?
e) Is the trigger clearly defined when it comes to you?
f) What could be done to improve the trigger's clarity?
g) What resources can be eliminated/ added/modified?

E. Look at **Feedback** for cause. Ask:
a) What further feedback during process steps is needed?
b) What feedback is further needed for inputs?
c) What feedback is further needed for conditions?
d) What feedback is missing or needed more when the work is finished?
e) Would a different schedule of reinforcement enhance desired results in inputs, conditions, process steps?
f) By whom should feedback be improved?
g) Is a system change needed for feedback?
h) Are there reports or automated reminders that would provide improved feedback?

F. Look at **Work Standards** for cause. Ask:
a) What standards need to be established/clarified?
b) Are standards ignored to get the work done?
c) Does the customer have stated/clear standard expectations?

G. Look at **Work Support** for cause. Ask:
a) What interventions, at what level, need improving or are missing?
b) What new interventions would improve work?
c) What interventions could be eliminated?
d) Are any interventions being ignored?
e) Do any interventions cause a barrier to work performance?

H. Look at **Human Relations** for cause. Ask:
a) What human relations factors are getting in the way of getting the work accomplished?
b) Does the human relations factor require professional help to fix?
c) Could policy changes improve Human Relations factors?

ORGANIZATIONAL SUPPORT

I. Look at **Financial Support** for cause. Ask:
a) What additional financial support is needed?
b) Is training require in financial literacy?
c) What additional financial support needs to be brought to the attention of senior management?

Answers The Question:
"How are work problems to be resolved?

Figure 37

to promote—for example, you may realize that "up-skilling" is necessary. The Work Analysis Aid merely confirms your intellectual and intuitive sense about going forward. It can be useful, too, in communicating to employees and your own management what you are doing and why.

The Work Analysis Aid also addresses other layers of work (work standards, work support, HR, and financial support) that may be influencing job and work group performance. The Language of Work is a robust tool that condenses all the various elements of work into its easily comprehensible series of charts and matrices. By applying your knowledge of your work and work force to these charts, you can integrate your thoughts and those of others into a coherent action plan understood by all.

While it may seem that continuous improvement is a complex addition to an already burdensome workload, in reality it is the essence of the manager's job. By looking at work execution and work support in terms of cause and effect, you are always looking to make work better for you, your employees, and the organization.

The alternative is unsatisfactory: just waiting for work problems to surface and trying to then do something. It never gets at the real issues that affect work. Not accounting for the fact that work issues are generally multidimensional; fixing one part without addressing others cannot lead to sustainable improvements. Continuous work improvement, as we have suggested here, helps avoid this piecemeal approach. With the Language of Work approach, the team can view work using a shared, commonly applied work language. Thus armed, they are equipped to identify and improve work based on the work models used to define both individual and group work. Identifying problems in the context of models allows discussions to take place with relatively little emotion. When changes are made, the information is easy to share. Using the other tools described above can engage everyone in other improvement efforts.

Welcome to a new and exciting Language of Work—one you share as executive, manager, and workers. Do let the authors know how you do.

Language of Work Terminology

Continuous Improvement

The programmatic mindset that is a natural extension of the Language of Work to improve work growing out of a fundamental understanding and execution of work using a Work Formula.

Human Relations

Those aspects of this work layer that recognize and support work execution promoted by an organization that seeks to make the work environment healthy in terms of human interactions in all levels of work execution.

Financial Support

Assuring that work execution has financial support through reasonable and appropriate funding.

Language of Work

A systemic, enterprise-wide behavioral model, based on the Work Formula, that integrates organizing, managing, implementing, and continuously improving work. In so doing it establishes alignment, transparency, and continuous improvement of work throughout an organization.

Work Alignment

Use of a Work Formula to align work levels and layers in terms of inputs, conditions, process steps, outputs, consequences, and feedback.

Work Analytics

Use of a Work Formula based on behavioral principles to systemically organize, manage, implement, and continuously improve work.

Work Analytic Tools

The variety of ways and means associated with operationalizing use of the Work Formula.

Work Formula

The six systemic elements that make up work; includes inputs, conditions, process steps, outputs, consequences, and feedback.

Work Layer

The aspects of work that are needed to support work execution; includes work standards, work support, human relations, and financial support.

Work Level

The work execution aspects of work that include business units, core processes, jobs, and work groups.

Work Matrices

The graphic representation of work layers using the Work Formula on one axis and the levels of work on the other. Each is populated with programs, services, and the like that represent the convergence of the axis in the matrix represented.

Work Models

Graphic flow diagram representations of the Work Formula designed to show business units, core processes, jobs, and work groups.

Work Standards

The layer of work to which work should rise in terms of quality, quantity, timeliness, and cost.

Work Support

The cultural provisions provided by an organization in direct support of work execution at the business unit, core processes, jobs, and work group levels.

Work Transparency

Assuring that the organization's work is defined operationally in terms of work levels and layers such that work entities, including job holders, teams, managers, and executives have clarity of work understanding, organization, facilitation, implementation, and continuous improvement.

Language of Work Implementation Models

The Managing Model has been addressed in this eBook. *The Business Model* and *The Working Model* are addressed in the two other eBooks of *The Work Trilogy.*

The following are the three major Work Implementation Models of the Language of Work. These are followed by a list of Organizational Effectiveness techniques that can use the Language of Work to improve their overall efficiency and effectiveness. You may access definitions, articles, case studies, books, and other information, including certification, at our website:

www.performanceinternational.com

Language of Work

The Business Model

For Executives

Work Formula

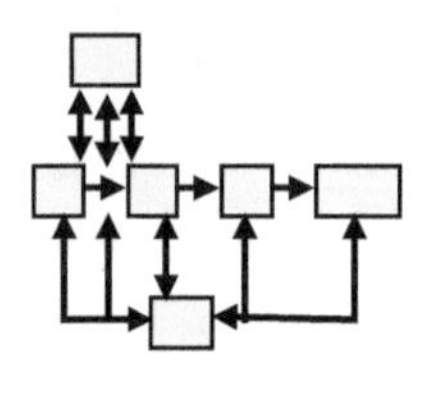

1. **Business Unit Model**
2. **Core Process Models**
3. **Job Models**
4. **Work Group Models**
5. **Work Standards Matrix**
6. **Work Support Matrix**
7. **Human Relations Matrix**
8. **Financial Support Matrix**

TO ACHIEVE:

- **Work Alignment**
- **Transparency**
- **Continuous Improvement**

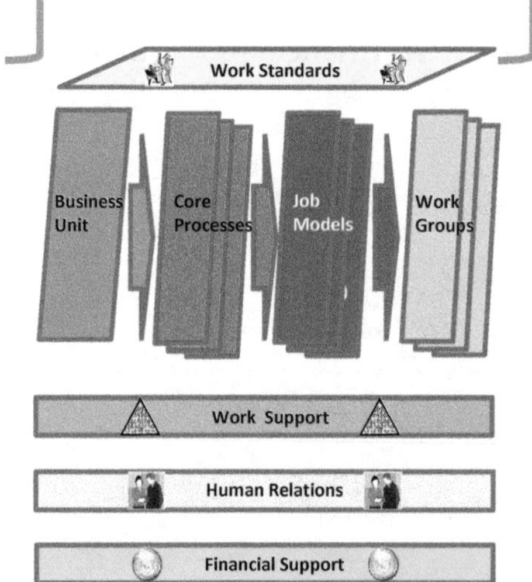

Language of Work
The Managing Model

For Managers

Work Formula

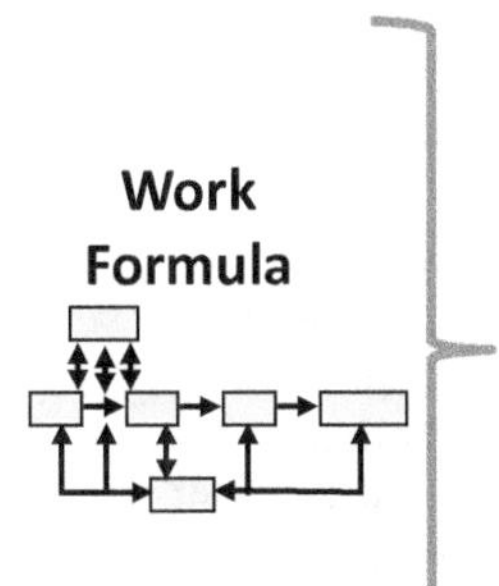

9. Planning Work
10. Linking With Other Groups
11. Selecting Employees
12. Job/Work Group Orientation
13. Establishing Systems
14. Assigning Tasks
15. Facilitating Work
16. Reinforcing Work Performance
17. Training & Work Performance
18. Facilitating Change
19. Facilitating Work Support
20. Informing Management
21. Job & Work Group Models
22. Assuring Role Relationships
23. Conducting Meetings
24. Improving Quality
25. Problem Solving
26. Resolving Conflicts
27. Measuring Work
28. Transferring Knowledge
29. Reviewing Performance
30. Career Development

TO ACHIEVE:

- Work Facilitation Alignment
- Transparency
- Continuous Improvement

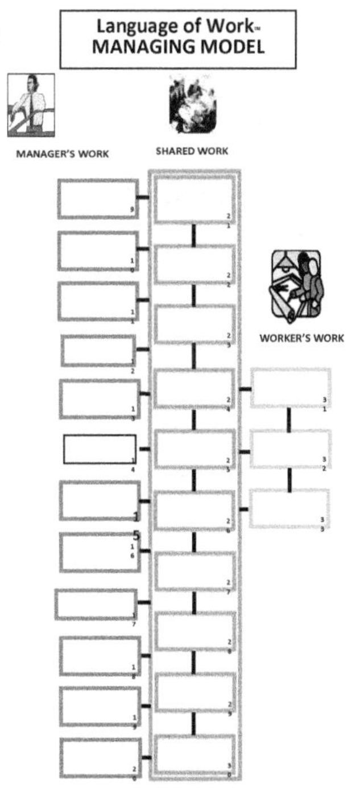

Language of Work

The Working Model

For Individual Worker and Team

Work Formula

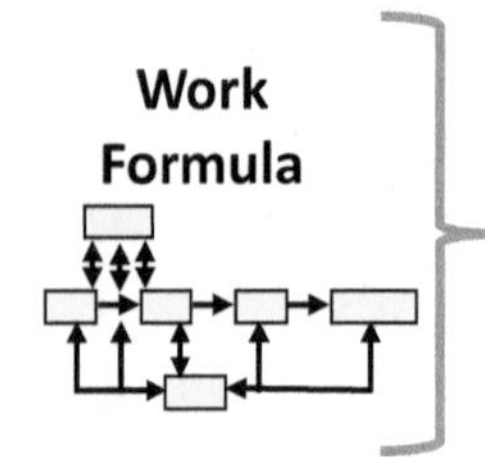

31. Work Implementation
32. Continuous Work Improvement

TO ACHIEVE:
- **Work Alignment**
- **Transparency**
- **Continuous Improvement**

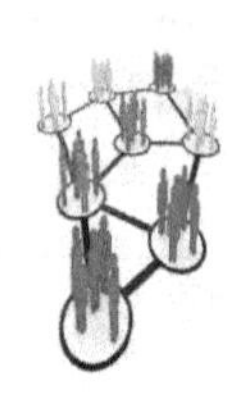

Organizational Effectiveness interventions that may be enhanced by use of the Language of Work Model:

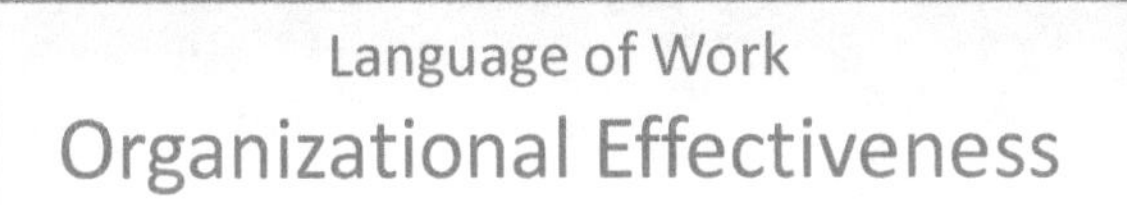

For:
Change Agents, Performance Consultants, Trainers, HR, etc

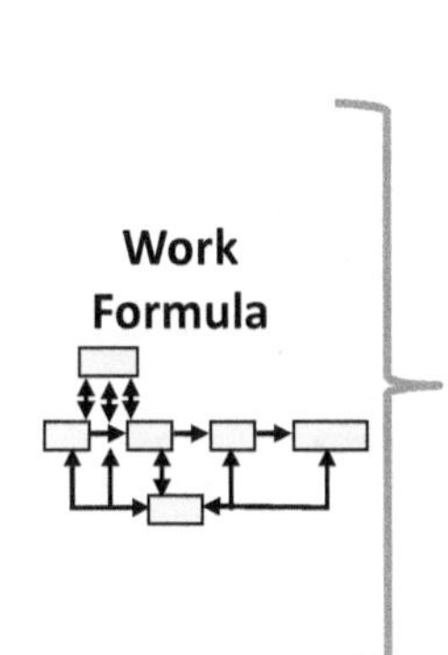

33. Integrated HR System
34. Competency Modeling
35. Re-engineering
36. Total Quality Management
37. Lean
38. Reorganization
39. Mergers
40. Acquisitions
41. New Business Start-up
42. Downsizing
43. Outsourcing
44. Expanding Operations
45. Training Needs Assessment & Development
46. Intervention Selection
47. Job Descriptions
48. Identifying & Loading Jobs to Core Processes

TO ACHIEVE:

- Systems Approach based on LoW
- Consistency with LoW Models

References

Hammer, Michael and James Champy. (1993) *Reengineering The Corporation*. New York: Harper-Collins.

Kolbe, K. (2003). *Powered By Instinct*. Phoenix, AZ: Monuments Press.

Langdon, Danny G. (2000). *Aligning Performance: Improving People, systems and Organizations.* San Francisco, CA: Jossey-Bass/Pheiffer Publishers.

Langdon, Danny G. (1995). *The New Language of Work*. Amherst, MA: HRD Press.

Langdon, Danny G. and Kathleen Whiteside, *Bringing Sense to Competency Definition and Attainment*, ISPI, Performance Improvement, vol. 43-7, 2004.

Langdon, Danny G., Kathleen Langdon, Johnilee Whiteside, (2014). *Righting the Enterprise – A Primer for Organizing or Reorganizing the Right Way.* Bellingham, WA: Performance International (free from our website at: http://lnkd.in/d66wnjb or in other formats at: https://www.smashwords.com/books/view/431840

Langdon, Danny G. (2001). *Should We Conduct Cause Analysis or Change of State Analysis*, ISPI, Performance Improvement, October, 2003, pp 8-13.

J. Robert Carlton and Claude S. Lineberry (2004). *Achieving Post-Merger Success.* San Francisco, CA: Jossey-Bass/Pheiffer Publishers.

Rummler, Geary A., and Alan P Brache. (1990) *Improving Performance: How to Manage the White Space on the Organization Chart* (2nd ed.). San Francisco, CA: Jossey-Bass/Pheiffer Publishers (p. 64).

LoW Books, Articles, YouTube, and Case Studies

Books

Langdon, Danny G. (1995) *The New Language of Work*. Amherst, MA: HRD Press.

Langdon, Danny G. (2000) *Aligning performance: Improving people, systems and organizations.* San Francisco, CA: Jossey-Bass/Pheiffer Publishers.

Langdon, Danny G., Kathleen Whiteside, and Monica McKenna. (1999). *Interventions Resource Guide: 50 Performance Improvement Tools.* San Francisco, CA: Jossey-Bass/Pheiffer Publishers.

Langdon, Danny G., Kathleen Langdon, Johnilee Whiteside, (2014) *Righting the Enterprise – A Primer for Organizing or Reorganizing the Right Way.* Bellingham, WA: Performance International (free from our website) at: http://lnkd.in/d66wnjb or in other formats at: https://www.smashwords.com/books/view/431840

Langdon, Danny G. and Kathleen Langdon. (2018) *The Work Trilogy: The Managing Model*: *Using The Language of Work To Facilitate Work,* Bellingham, WA: Performance International, www.performanceinternational.com.

Langdon, Danny G. and Kathleen Langdon. (2018) *The Work Trilogy: The Working Model*: *Using The Language of Work To Implement Work,* Bellingham, WA: Performance International, www.performanceinternational.com.

LoW Related Articles

Langdon, D.G. A new language of work, Quality Digest, Oct., 1994 44-48.

Langdon, D.G. Aligning performance: the ultimate goal of our profession, Performance Improvement Journal, vol. 39, no. 3, 22-26.

Langdon, D.G. Redefining jobs and work in changing organizations, HR Magazine, May, 1996, 97-101.

Langdon, D.G. Return of the craftsman, Unpublished article, available from Performance International.

Langdon, D.G. Self-directed TQM, Unpublished article, available from Performance International..

Langdon, D.G. and Anne F. Marrelli. A new model for systemic competency identification, ISPI Journal, vol. 41, no. 4, 14-21.

Langdon, D.G. reOrganizing your department in 9 steps, Concept Paper, available from Performance International.

Langdon, D.G. Improving management communication through job models, ISPI Journal, vol. 55, no. 7, 17-18.

LoW YouTube Sources

10-Minute Teach: https://youtu.be/Nn7tLm4nRLU

Business Optimization Dashboard: http://www.youtube.com/watch?v=WhS2KMdHm70

YouTube Chats on the Language of Work:

Title	URL
Introduction: Conversations with the Model Maker	https://youtu.be/n8_qrI4S8iQ
Historical Context	https://youtu.be/eToNViGfRqQ
Why Did You Create the Language of Work?	https://youtu.be/mhTXUaZsel4
Essential Elements of Work: Formula Models	https://youtu.be/eRwpkM0VoBk
Work Formula	https://youtu.be/pjmudw2iojY
Work as a System	https://youtu.be/hFpjgo9KuJs
Use of Language of Work for Individuals (Job Model)	https://youtu.be/GBNczPhNxgU
Language of Work and Reorganizations	https://youtu.be/wvzrzed-pVc
Who Does What in Job Modeling?	https://youtu.be/kJ0o8-6ASXc
Why Two Facilitators?	https://youtu.be/pewSTjet1yM
Skills of Data Gatherer in LOW	https://youtu.be/b_gmbwScdgI
Why Not Brainstorm?	https://youtu.be/OeLSoLOQ4xw
Resistance to Language of Work	https://youtu.be/h_CJorkC6rI
Interface with Human Resources	https://youtu.be/wChyHGHg2wU
Handling Resistance	https://youtu.be/paKRrBHr4Xk
Finite Set of Data for Organizational Development	https://youtu.be/7lckhpbSfic
Improve Organizational Development Practice	https://youtu.be/7YR-4iB25lo

LoW Related Case Studies

Case Studies are available from PerformanceInternational.com and demonstrate various applications of the Language of Work Model:

AQUA Company—Reorganization

The Information Technology (IT) Department at a major water utility had grown like topsy-turvy over a ten-year period, losing credibility with clients and senior management because of its expensive inability to deliver on a promise to develop its own enterprise-wide software. In desperation, after spending many millions of dollars on a non-deliverable, senior management purchased and installed a commercial ERP (SAP) software package. A unit was created to tailor and install the new software, which did not report to the centralized IT department.

A survey showed that 250 people performed IT functions within AQUA, but fewer than 100 reported to the centralized IT unit. The others were spread over several operating departments, and the SAP unit. In other words, like many organizations today, IT was both centralized and decentralized. Senior management wanted to know whether this was the optimal organizational structure; if not, why not, and how any new, proposed structure would compare to other similar companies.

College Student-Centric Studies—Organizational Alignment

A junior college in the Midwest (U.S.) had completed a reorganization (not using the Language of Work model) to reduce the number of administrators, to enhance the registration and financial aid processes, and to reduce personnel costs. The primary goals of the consolidation were to result in increased enrollment, higher student achievement and improved reputation of the college. Once the cuts had been made, it became clear that additional work was needed to understand operationally (a core process) how to achieve goals of being student-centric. It was also clear that the jobs within the new department would also need to change. Specifically, they needed to develop a student-centered process, creating an improved flow for students (including single-stop registration) and enhanced productivity of staff. Finally, improved communication between and among faculty, Student Services staff and students was critical in solving problems and removing obstacles for students to continue school to graduate and increase enrollment.

Defense Contractor—Changing a Corporate Strategy

A great challenge occurs when an enterprise decides, for very good business reasons, to change the strategy it has pursued for years, perhaps since its inception. Ideas are great, and strategic planning sessions are exciting and invigorating. However, it is when the operational aspects of a new strategy must be planned, changed, recruited and trained for seamlessly that trouble can begin. This case study shows a systematic way of translating strategy into operational excellence using the Language of Work Model.

Government Case Study—Culture Change

A government agency outsourced operations and revenue collection to a private company. It became clear that parties on both sides had experienced frustration with the "way things are." Executives in both organizations came to realize that the different cultures of the two organizations had interfered with optimal performance. Both parties wanted to ensure the future relationship would be a model for privatization contracts across North America. A cultural audit would provide the data, analysis and recommendations to help employees of both organizations understand the other and achieve high performance standards.

Hi Tech Case Study—Core Process Improvement

The ability of any organization to protect its employees and its intellectual property from hackers is vital today. The Language of Work™ model for reorganizing allowed this unit to look at all the technical aspects of ensuring IT security while keeping a clear eye on how to get the work done, and aligning the organization's jobs to its core work.

Life Insurance Case Study—Cultural Change

After years of poor management, a new president took over a division of a large insurance company which was losing market share and profitability. He knew he had a short honeymoon period in which to turn the organization around. He selected the authors to aid him because they had a good performance (work) improvement model and could work at all the levels of the organization. They worked closely with him and his management team to define the current and desired state of the business unit, the core processes, the individual jobs, and the work groups—completing all the performance improvement in sixty days.

Major Utility Case Study— Core Process to Jobs Improvement

The change in weather patterns is placing extreme demands on the utilities and fire departments around the US. An autumn fifty-year snowstorm that followed a devastating hurricane just sixty days earlier caused so much damage that residents and businesses were without electricity for as many as twelve days. The utility was forced to analyze and repair its emergency management system. Analysis using the LoW process model allowed 25 different agencies to develop a coordinated plan to respond to future emergencies.

New Enterprise—New Global Business Formation

The author of this case study is a user of the Language of Work in a global startup. He points to the multiple uses he has made of the LoW model, capturing the essence of the performance aspect of the model. The author can thus see and align the many organizations he is creating because the LoW mirrors what the work of the business will be. He has been "testing" the claims and value of the Language of Work by using it in multiple real-life settings.

Nursing Services—Nonprofit Problem Solving

A nonprofit organization had a new executive director. The agency provided nursing support in homes and in jails, as well as light housekeeping for certain clients. She was aware of myriad financial, reputational and performance problems in the organization she was heading but needed a path for resolving them. By using the LoW AS IS/TO BE Work Analytic Tool, a series of actionable steps were captured for making needed work and cultural changes.

Author Biographies

Danny G. Langdon, Co-founder of Performance International, with forty+ years' experience, has published twelve books, and served as the series editor of the 40-volume "Instructional Designs Library." He is the recipient of three major ISPI awards of excellence, a past international president, and Honorary Life Member. He is the originator of the Language of Work Model,™ and has presented at more than 35 international conferences, published numerous articles, and conducted numerous workshops.

Kathleen Langdon, Co-founder of Performance International, has served external clients for more than thirty years, concentrating on embedding work performance improvement in numerous companies. She served as Corporate Director of Human Resources for a major service medical organization. She is a past president of ISPI, invited speaker for the annual ISPI Awards Banquet, and led 15 business executives to explain performance technology to the White House. She is the co-editor of "Intervention Resource Guide: 50 Performance Improvement Tools," published numerous articles, and is a frequent presenter at conferences here and abroad.

CPSIA information can be obtained
at www.ICGtesting.com
Printed in the USA
FSHW01n0326060818
51036FS

9 780991 397587